D0821600

Blackwell Essential Literature

Romantic Poetry

Edited by Duncan Wu

Blackwell
Publishing

Copyright © 2002 by Blackwell Publishers Ltd
a Blackwell Publishing company

Editorial matter, selection and arrangement copyright ©
Duncan Wu 2002

Editorial Offices:
108 Cowley Road, Oxford OX4 1JF, UK
Tel: +44 (0)1865 791100
350 Main Street, Malden,
MA 02148-5018, USA
Tel: +1 781 388 8250

First published 2002 by Blackwell Publishers Ltd.

Library of Congress Cataloging-in-Publication Data

Romantic poetry
p. cm.—(Blackwell essential literature)
Includes bibliographical references and index.
ISBN 0-631-22973-6 (alk. paper)—ISBN 0-631-22974-4 (pbk.: alk. paper)
1. English poetry—19th century. 2. English poetry—18th century. 3.
Romanticism—Great Britain. I. Wu, Duncan. II. Series.
PR1222 .R65 2002   821'. 7080145—dc21   2002020873

A catalogue record for this title is available from the British Library

Set in 8/10pt Galliard
by Kolam Information Services Pvt. Ltd, Pondicherry, India
Printed and bound at T.J. International Ltd, Padstow, Cornwall

For further information on
Blackwell Publishers, visit our website:
www.blackwellpublishers.com

Contents

William Wordsworth (1770–1850)

Samuel Taylor Coleridge (1772–1834)

Series Editor's Preface

The Blackwell Essential Literature series offers readers the chance to possess authoritative texts of key poems (and in one case drama) across the standard periods and movements. Based on correspondent volumes in the Blackwell Anthologies series, most of these volumes run to no more than 200 pages. The acknowledged virtues of the Blackwell Anthologies are range and variety; those of the Essential Literature series are authoritative selection, compactness and ease of use. They will be particularly helpful to students hard-pressed for time, who need a digest of the poetry of each historical period.

In selecting the contents of each volume particular attention has been given to major writers whose works are widely taught at most schools and universities. Each volume contains a general introduction designed to introduce the reader to those central works.

Together, these volumes comprise a crucial resource for anyone who reads or studies poetry.

Duncan Wu
St Catherine's College, Oxford

Introduction

Duncan Wu

Even the Romantics could not agree on a definition of Romanticism. At the time *Lyrical Ballads* appeared in 1798 it meant 'fanciful', 'light', even 'inconsequential'. Wordsworth and Coleridge would have resisted its application, and, twenty years later, the second generation of romantic writers recognized it only as part of a debate among European intellectuals. On one level, of course, that's the way of literary discourse; critical debates (even when conducted by practitioners) don't always bear on the practical business of writing.

Romance was once used to refer to the verse epics of Tasso and Ariosto. Later critics used it in relation to fiction, and it was in that context that Novalis applied it to German literature. But the idea didn't take off until August Wilhelm Schlegel exploited it in a lecture course he delivered at Berlin in 1801–4. Romantic literature, he argued, appeared in the Middle Ages with the work of Dante, Petrarch and Boccaccio. To him, it was identified with progressive and Christian views. In another course of lectures in Vienna, 1808–9, he went further: Romanticism was 'organic' and 'plastic', as against the 'mechanical' tendencies of Classicism. This was the beginning of an argument that continues to this day. Put crudely, it raises the question of how 'high' Romanticism was related to the literature and thought of the Enlightenment period in the eighteenth century.

Not only does Romanticism remain difficult – some would say impossible to define, but the poets in this book would not have seen themselves as a unified or coherent body. They never met in the same room and, had they done so, would have fallen out. Why? For one thing, there was a generation gap. Byron, Shelley and Keats might have enjoyed the company of Wordsworth as he had been in his twenties and early thirties, for they regarded his greatest work as *Tintern Abbey* and the 'Ode'. But by the time they reached artistic maturity – *c.*1816 for Shelley and Byron, 1819 for Keats – he had become the lost leader who had accepted the job of Distributor of Stamps for Westmoreland, supported corrupt Tory interests in the election of 1818, and abandoned the radical convictions of his youth. 'He is a slave', Mary Shelley confided to her journal in 1814. Nor did they know of *The Prelude* – a work that confirms Wordsworth's genius, and bears out some of his earlier aspirations – which remained unpublished until its author's death in 1850.

Blake is the eldest of the poets here, born in 1757, a full 12 years before Wordsworth. He may have been a product of the Enlightenment but was opposed to its positivistic, rationalist tendencies. As a young man in London he saw angels in the trees on Peckham Rye and ghosts in

Westminster Abbey. Instead of going to university he was apprenticed to an engraver, and illustration work provided him with an income for the rest of his life. That expertise also gave him the means by which to produce books in an unusual manner of his own devising. His 'infernal' method consisted of drawing texts and designs onto a copper plate with a varnish resistant to the corrosive effects of acid. Each plate would be hand-printed and the page coloured individually, by him or his wife, in watercolour. Anyone wishing to buy one of his books would have to go to his house and order it personally. This uncommercial manner of publication meant that he produced few copies during his lifetime, and lived and died in impoverished obscurity.

That may have been as well, because as an intensely visionary writer Blake was deemed wayward (even mad) by those who did read him. Some of his most ambitious writings – *Milton*, *Jerusalem*, *Vala* – featured characters (or emanations) roughly equivalent to such abstract forces as reason (Urizen), revolution (Orc) and imagination (Los). But there's nothing schematic about Blake's world or the way in which his emanations behave.

His *Songs of Innocence and Experience* (1789–94), presented here entire, include his most accessible works. When producing copies for patrons, Blake occasionally varied the order of the poems and even moved some from one book to the other, indicating that he believed the organizing principles of innocence and experience to be not in opposition but in dialogue. They include some of the greatest short poems of the period, including 'London', 'The Sick Rose', 'The Garden of Love', 'The Divine Image' and 'The Tyger'.

It says a good deal for Wordsworth that in 1812 he said he considered Blake 'as having the elements of poetry a thousand times more than either Byron or Scott' – high praise from someone parsimonious with compliments. By that time Wordsworth had become known for *Lyrical Ballads* (1798, second edition 1800) and *Poems in Two Volumes* (1807). It is a curious fact that the poem now considered to be his greatest achievement, *The Prelude*, though completed in two Parts in 1799, and revised in Thirteen Books in 1805, remained in manuscript until after his death in 1850. It was therefore unknown to all but his closest friends. Wordsworth saw it as the prelude to his great epic 'The Recluse', which he believed would alter the social and political constitution of the world by revealing how love of nature leads to love of mankind. He hoped that process would bring about an egalitarian society without distinction of status or property. Unfortunately he would never write 'The Recluse' (and perhaps no one could have done), but we do at least have its prelude – a work that tells the story of Wordsworth's life to explain how he arrived at his vocation. *The Two-Part Prelude* is its earliest version, of which Part I is presented here complete. Begun in what Wordsworth believed to be the coldest winter of the century, it begins with a despairing question, 'Was it for this . . .?', as he asks why he finds himself unable to write 'The Recluse'.

It is distinguished for many passages that demonstrate the significance of memory and imagination in Wordsworth's thinking and disprove the notion that he saw nature as a wholly beneficent force. In the spots of time in Part I he is guided by natural forces that used 'Severer interventions, ministry/More palpable'. By this he means that they educated him by submitting him to sublime experiences that continued to haunt him. The wait for the horses to take him and his brothers home to see his dying father, for instance, left a series of sense-impressions impressed on his memory, to which he returned 'and thence would drink/As at a fountain'. These experiences are not pleasant: one concerns a drowned man, another deals with intense feelings of guilt at stealing a boat, and yet another describes feelings of dislocation, alienation and emotional intensity at being lost in a strange place. In the end, Wordsworth's poetry is less preoccupied with nature than with the workings of the mind.

Coleridge helped Wordsworth formulate 'The Recluse' and was closely associated with him during a productive period for them both – 1797–8. During that year, besides working on 'The Recluse', they composed *Lyrical Ballads* (1798) which contained *The Ancient Mariner*. This is one of the most compelling poems of the Romantic age, both because Coleridge handles the ballad form with such skill, and because its story continues to haunt us long after the poem is finished. Critics continue to argue over its meaning, some take its concluding moral as a straightforward utterance of faith, but many find it hard to reconcile with the relentless damnation described by the mariner. What else is he, they ask, but an ordinary man who in a thoughtless moment committed a crime (and a fairly trivial one at that) against the natural world? The consequences, not merely for him, but for many innocent people too, are out of proportion to the act. Is it the business of a benevolent Deity to condemn him to an unending journey that brings devastation and misery to those he encounters? Is there a God in the poem at all? Or is Coleridge more concerned with a metaphorical explication of original sin and its consequences?

Whatever the answers, *The Ancient Mariner* seems to describe a kind of spiritual hell, something that recurs in Coleridge's other works in this selection. Her name composed of those of two suffering innocents from the Bible, Christ Abel brings evil upon herself by an act of common kindness – the taking-in of Geraldine. Her reward hardly seems appropriate, for Geraldine is a lamia – half-woman, half-serpent – whose aim is to transfer her 'contaminated' nature to the innocent Christabel. This too is a story that seems to throw into question the just world heralded by 'The Recluse'. Perhaps, having devised Wordsworth's great epic, Coleridge had begun to lose faith in it. If so, his doubt could not have been channelled to greater creative effect. Part I only is presented here, which Coleridge wrote in February 1798. Two years later he wrote a second Part, which described the effects on Christabel of the night spent with Geraldine – loss of her power of speech, among other things. It appears, with a summary of how the poem might have concluded, in *Romanticism: An Anthology* (2nd edn), pp. 483–90 (listed in suggested reading below).

Kubla Khan is an inspired account of the creative impulse. A ruthless military man he may have been, but Kubla's ambitions in creating a para-disal world in Xanadu are hardly to be condemned. Despite the pleasure we may take in the creative exuberance of the 'mighty fountain', however, the

'Ancestral voices prophecying war' articulate a tendency from deep within. And they will not be banished. The implication is clear: for all our desires to create a better, fairer world, for all our dreams of paradise, the human soul is given to evil courses. But is this necessarily to be regretted? The last section of the poem provides a sort of answer. The vision of the damsel with a dulcimer is bewitching but cannot be 'revived'. Coleridge seems to realize that, unfortunate though this is, it would drive him mad were it to return. *Kubla Khan* takes the Romantic ideal of the transcendent vision and asks whether, along with being difficult (if not impossible) to attain, it might also be undesirable.

Although written during 1797–8 *Kubla Khan* and *Christabel* were not published until 1816, at the insistence of Lord Byron. Born with a deformed foot and lame throughout his life, Byron was 'differently abled' only in the sense that he made others seem inert by comparison. A hereditary peer at the age of ten, he led a rebellion against his headmaster at Harrow, scored 18 runs in the Eton–Harrow cricket match before he left, kept a tame bear in his rooms at Cambridge, swam the Tagus in 1809 and the Hellespont the following year, and throughout his life had love affairs with partners of both sexes, not least his half-sister Augusta Leigh, whom he described as the one true love of his life. It would be easy to argue that such an existence was a mammoth act of compensation – and perhaps it was – but one suspects that even without his disability Byron would have been thrown into the limelight.

He came to prominence in 1812 when he began publishing *Childe Harold's Pilgrimage*, an autobiographical work about the doings of his *alter ego*, Childe Harold, whose melancholy ruminations generated endless intrigue among its readers. Its success made Byron an overnight celebrity in whose life the public took the same kind of interest now reserved for film stars and pop singers. Lurid tales of his private life proliferated, especially when his divorced wife Annabella Milbanke told the world of his homosexual youth. Such revelations were unlikely to discourage the horrified interest of his fans; on the contrary, they stoked the public appetite for more. By the time his publisher John Murray began to issue *Don Juan* in 1819 every copy of the large run would be sure to sell, and subsequent editions called for within weeks if not days. The poem would turn out to be Byron's masterpiece, and he would work on it until his death in 1824 when it was left unfinished.

Of *Don Juan* he declared: 'I *have* no plan – I *had* no plan – but I had or have materials', and the manner in which it is written is just as important as its story – as he observed, 'I mean it for a poetical *Tristram Shandy*'. No one in their right mind would read it primarily for its plot, so filled is it with digression. But that was the point: it possesses all the waywardness, unpredictability and accumulated detritus of life as lived – something conveyed in Canto II, which is presented here entire.

The reaction of its first readers was one of confused horror, for Byron deliberately set out to confront contemporary taboos. The shipwreck scene was a principal source of unease, as the reviewer in the *British Critic* declared:

In the scenes of confusion and agony attending a shipwreck, in the struggles for self-preservation, in the loss of so many souls, perhaps but too unprepared for their great account, in tracing the protracted sufferings of those whose lot is still to linger on in desperation drearier than death, in viewing a company of fellow-creatures on the wide ocean, devouring their last morsel, in witnessing hunger and thirst increasing upon them, the cannibal passions beginning to rise, the casting of lots for destruction, the self-immolation, the feast upon human blood, the frantic feeling of satiety – surely in bringing all these things home to our hearts, we can ill endure a full-born jest. Much less can we tolerate the mixing up of these fearful events with low doggerel and vapid absurdity.

One could hardly argue that the shipwreck was not intended to be realistic: Byron based it on documentary evidence. What upset the reviewer most was the pleasure Byron took in exposing the animalistic urges that, he claimed, underlay social behaviour ('... man is a carnivorous production/ And must have meals, at least one meal a day'). A less honest writer might have had the inhabitants of the lifeboat pray for salvation and receive sustenance, but Byron took undisguised pleasure in ensuring that Juan's tutor Pedrillo, licensed to perform religious rites, got eaten by the crew. As if this was not enough, he then had those who had dined on Pedrillo go mad, implying a connection between religious belief and dementia. In *Don Juan* nothing is exempt from ridicule, even young love. That between Haidée and Juan is encouraged by breakfast because, Byron says, 'the best feelings must have victual'.

Byron believed passionately in revolutionary ideals, and it is typical that his maiden speech in the House of Lords (the secondary chamber in the British Houses of Parliament) was in support of Luddite frame-breakers. Of the six poets represented here, all of whom sympathized at some point with radical beliefs, he was the only one to die in a revolution, fighting in the Greek war of independence. (He remains a national hero in Greece today.) His friend Percy Bysshe Shelley shared those convictions throughout his life. From the outset Shelley detested what he regarded as the corrupt status of the established church (which at that time had real political power), and as an undergraduate at Oxford was sent down for writing a pamphlet in favour of atheism. A year later he went to Dublin and wrote and campaigned in favour of Catholic emancipation and the repeal of the Act of Union. Back in England he came under the influence of William Godwin, the precursor of nineteenth-century socialism and forerunner of Karl Marx. In 1816 he eloped with Godwin's daughter Mary to the Continent where they encountered Byron, who had just gone into voluntary exile. That summer, on the shores of Lake Geneva, they forged a creative partnership that inspired *Mont Blanc* and *Hymn to Intellectual Beauty*, as well as Mary's novel *Frankenstein*.

Mont Blanc can be read as a response to *Tintern Abbey*, in which Wordsworth had written confidently of 'A motion and a spirit that impels/All thinking things, all objects of all thought,/And rolls through all things'. Likewise, Shelley hopes that the 'still and solemn Power' of the natural world can 'repeal/Large codes of fraud and woe'. The idea that some unnamed power in nature could neutralize the self-interested tendencies of earthly rulers must have seemed absurd at a time when kings could declare wars, raise taxes and dissolve governments. All the same, it was one that Shelley held, and was consistent with his conviction that poetry was an agent for political change: poets, he wrote in 1821, 'are the un-acknowledged legislators of the world'. In 1816 he is capable of questioning his beliefs as well as declaring them, and at the end of *Mont Blanc* he asks the mountain

> And what were thou, and earth, and stars, and sea,
> If to the human mind's imaginings
> Silence and solitude were vacancy?

Wordsworth would not have approved. Such gestures were typical of the subversive, sceptical spirit that led Shelley to take pleasure in describing himself in hotel registers as 'atheist and democrat' (equivalent to 'communist' in 1950s America) – something that shocked even Byron.

Shelley was not really an atheist (at least not as we understand the term) and did not truly regard his mind's imaginings as 'vacancy'. There were times when he wrote without ironizing his beliefs, as when he heard of the Peterloo Massacre. He had been travelling for about a year in Italy when the news arrived. On 16 August 1819, at St Peter's Field, on the outskirts of Manchester, a political meeting of 60,000 working men and women had been brutally dispersed by mounted dragoons with a brutality that left (according to conservative official figures) 11 people dead and 421 cases of serious injury (including more than 100 women and children and 162 individual cases of sabre wounds). Unofficial figures were higher. Within twelve days Shelley composed one of the greatest poems of political protest in the language. *The Mask of Anarchy* begins with fierce satire, depicting the ministers of Lord Liverpool's government riding the horses which trample the crowd; from stanzas 34 to 63, a maid who has risen up to halt Anarchy (the idol of both the government and the people) addresses them, distinguishing between false and true freedom; in the concluding section she tells them to stand up for their rights using passive, non-violent demonstration.

Shelley posted the poem to Leigh Hunt for publication in his journal, *The Examiner*, but these were repressive times and Hunt was afraid to publish. He had been imprisoned for libelling the Prince Regent in 1813 and was not anxious to repeat the experience. He was right. *The Mask of Anarchy* would have been regarded as treasonable at a time when people could be fined or tried for a single word. It remained in manuscript until published in 1832 to coincide with the passing of the Reform Bill.

Shelley wrote *Ode to the West Wind* just over a month after *The Mask of Anarchy* – which would suggest that it is more than just a nature poem. It is also a statement of faith in the aspiration to resist the oppressions of church and state, and become self-determining: 'Pestilence-stricken multitudes' are thus bidden to participate in the millennial vision of 'a new birth'. Shelley insists on the prophet-like status of the poet, 'tameless, and swift, and proud', who will awaken the masses to the possibility of revolution: 'Drive my dead thoughts over the universe/Like withered leaves to quicken a new birth!' (ll. 63–4). It is his most cogent expression of political and spiritual aspiration.

Of these poets, Keats was the last born and the first to die – at the early age of 26. Had the others died so young, we would probably regard them as minor and of little significance. Keats developed very quickly – and seems to have suspected that he needed to, in his short life producing some of the finest poetry of his day. This selection includes the odes of 1819 which remain his crowning achievement. They use forms designed to enable him to explore lines of thought across several stanzas while retaining the discipline of a sonnet. At the same time, he is subject to none of the constraints of conventional narrative. With all these advantages, Keats was free to exploit an authorial voice – not always a confident one (as Wordsworth's had been) – which could ask big questions without necessarily finding answers. Love, death, transience, loss, beauty, the creative imagination, and the aspiration towards a transcendent vision – these are the subjects of the odes.

The Eve of St Agnes is among the best of his narrative works. It reflects his admiration of Byron's *Don Juan* and growing desire to write 'only for men'. To that end he revised it before publication to heighten elements he hoped would upset and alienate his largely female readership – the deaths of Angela and the beadsman, and the sexual encounter at the centre of the poem. He succeeded in creating a work that would appeal strongly to such writers as Tennyson and the Pre-Raphaelites.

While it would be mistaken to regard the Romantics as a coherent group in the same sense as the Imagists in the early twentieth century, it is true that they were products of a common *zeitgeist*. The age was one of rapid and violent political change in which ordinary people realized – for the first time – that they not only had a voice but rights as well. The American and French Revolutions were indications of that change, and after the Napoleonic Wars the long struggle towards enfranchisement could begin. It is true that by 1820 Wordsworth and Coleridge were no longer the firebrands they had been in the 1790s, but the poetry they had written in earlier years led Byron, Shelley and Keats, at various stages, to believe that they were inheritors of a tradition that Wordsworth and Coleridge had initiated. This brief selection is an attempt to illustrate some aspects of that new way of thinking which continues to shape our literature today.

Further Reading

Wu, Duncan (ed.) (1996) *Romanticism: A Critical Reader* (Oxford: Blackwell).

Wu, Duncan (ed.) (1997) *Romantic Women Poets: An Anthology* (Oxford: Blackwell).

Wu, Duncan (ed.) (1998) *A Companion to Romanticism* (Oxford: Blackwell).

Wu, Duncan (ed.) (2001) *Romanticism: An Anthology with CD-ROM*, 2nd edn (Oxford: Blackwell).

William Blake (1757–1827)

Introduction

Piping down the valleys wild,
Piping songs of pleasant glee,
On a cloud I saw a child
And he laughing said to me:

'Pipe a song about a lamb!'   5
So I piped with a merry cheer;
'Piper, pipe that song again!'
So I piped – he wept to hear.

'Drop thy pipe, thy happy pipe,
Sing thy songs of happy cheer!'   10
So I sung the same again
While he wept with joy to hear.

'Piper, sit thee down and write
In a book, that all may read.'
So he vanished from my sight   15
And I plucked a hollow reed.

And I made a rural pen,
And I stained the water clear,
And I wrote my happy songs
Every child may joy to hear.   20

The Shepherd

How sweet is the shepherd's sweet lot!
From the morn to the evening he strays;
He shall follow his sheep all the day
And his tongue shall be filled with praise.

For he hears the lamb's innocent call,   5
And he hears the ewe's tender reply;
He is watchful while they are in peace,
For they know when their shepherd is nigh.

The Echoing Green

The sun does arise
And make happy the skies;
The merry bells ring
To welcome the spring;
The skylark and thrush,   5
The birds of the bush,
Sing louder around
To the bells' cheerful sound,
While our sports shall be seen
On the echoing green.   10

Old John with white hair
Does laugh away care,
Sitting under the oak
Among the old folk,
They laugh at our play   15
And soon they all say,
'Such, such were the joys
When we all, girls and boys,
In our youth-time were seen
On the echoing green.'   20

Till the little ones weary
No more can be merry,
The sun does descend
And our sports have an end;
Round the laps of their mothers,   25
Many sisters and brothers
Like birds in their nest
Are ready for rest,
And sport no more seen
On the darkening green.   30

The Lamb

Little lamb, who made thee?
Dost thou know who made thee?
Gave thee life and bid thee feed
By the stream and o'er the mead;

Gave thee clothing of delight –   5
Softest clothing, woolly, bright;
Gave thee such a tender voice,
Making all the vales rejoice?
　　Little lamb, who made thee?
　　Dost thou know who made thee?   10

　　Little lamb, I'll tell thee,
　　Little lamb, I'll tell thee;
He is called by thy name,
For he calls himself a lamb;
He is meek and he is mild,   15
He became a little child:
I a child and thou a lamb,
We are called by his name.
　　Little lamb, God bless thee,
　　Little lamb, God bless thee.   20

The Little Black Boy

My mother bore me in the southern wild
And I am black, but oh, my soul is white!
White as an angel is the English child,
But I am black, as if bereaved of light.

My mother taught me underneath a tree,   5
And sitting down before the heat of day,
She took me on her lap and kissed me,
And pointing to the east began to say,

'Look on the rising run: there God does live,
And gives his light, and gives his heat away;   10
And flowers and trees and beasts and men receive
Comfort in morning, joy in the noonday.

And we are put on earth a little space
That we may learn to bear the beams of love;
And these black bodies and this sunburnt face   15
Is but a cloud, and like a shady grove.

For when our souls have learned the heat to bear
The cloud will vanish; we shall hear his voice
Saying, "Come out from the grove, my love and care,
And round my golden tent like lambs rejoice!"'   20

Thus did my mother say, and kissed me;
And thus I say to little English boy,

When I from black and he from white cloud free,
And round the tent of God like lambs we joy,

I'll shade him from the heat, till he can bear   25
To lean in joy upon our Father's knee;
And then I'll stand and stroke his silver hair,
And be like him, and he will then love me.

The Blossom

Merry merry sparrow
Under leaves so green!
A happy blossom
Sees you swift as arrow;
Seek your cradle narrow   5
Near my bosom.

Pretty pretty robin
Under leaves so green!
A happy blossom
Hears you sobbing, sobbing,   10
Pretty pretty robin,
Near my bosom.

The Chimney Sweeper

When my mother died I was very young,
And my father sold me while yet my tongue
Could scarcely cry 'weep weep weep weep!'
So your chimneys I sweep, and in soot I sleep.

There's little Tom Dacre, who cried when his head,   5
That curled like a lamb's back, was shaved; so I said,
'Hush, Tom! Never mind it, for when your head's bare
You know that the soot cannot spoil your white hair.'

And so he was quiet, and that very night,
As Tom was a-sleeping, he had such a sight!   10
That thousands of sweepers – Dick, Joe, Ned and Jack,
Were all of them locked up in coffins of black.

And by came an angel who had a bright key,
And he opened the coffins and set them all free;
Then down a green plain leaping, laughing they run   15
And wash in a river, and shine in the sun.

Then naked and white, all their bags left behind,
They rise upon clouds and sport in the wind;
And the angel told Tom, if he'd be a good boy,
He'd have God for his father and never want joy.   20

And so Tom awoke, and we rose in the dark,
And got with our bags and our brushes to work;
Though the morning was cold, Tom was happy and warm –
So if all do their duty, they need not fear harm.

The Little Boy Lost

'Father, father, where are you going?
Oh do not walk so fast!
Speak, father, speak to your little boy
Or else I shall be lost.'

The night was dark, no father was there,   5
The child was wet with dew;
The mire was deep, and the child did weep,
And away the vapour flew.

The Little Boy Found

The little boy lost in the lonely fen,
Led by the wand'ring light,
Began to cry; but God, ever nigh,
Appeared like his father in white.

He kissed the child, and by the hand led,   5
And to his mother brought,
Who in sorrow pale, through the lonely dale
Her little boy weeping sought.

Laughing Song

When the green woods laugh with the voice of joy,
And the dimpling stream runs laughing by;
When the air does laugh with our merry wit,
And the green hill laughs with the noise of it;

When the meadows laugh with lively green,   5
And the grasshopper laughs in the merry scene;
When Mary and Susan and Emily
With their sweet round mouths sing, 'Ha, ha, he!'

When the painted birds laugh in the shade,
Where our table with cherries and nuts is spread,   10
Come live and be merry, and join with me
To sing the sweet chorus of 'Ha, ha, he!'

A Cradle Song

Sweet dreams, form a shade
O'er my lovely infant's head;
Sweet dreams of pleasant streams
By happy, silent, moony beams.

Sweet sleep, with soft down   5
Weave thy brows an infant crown;
Sweet sleep, angel mild,
Hover o'er my happy child.

Sweet smiles in the night
Hover over my delight;   10
Sweet smiles, mother's smiles,
All the livelong night beguiles.

Sweet moans, dovelike sighs,
Chase not slumber from thy eyes;
Sweet moans, sweeter smiles,   15
All the dovelike moans beguiles.

Sleep, sleep, happy child,
All creation slept and smiled;
Sleep, sleep, happy sleep,
While o'er thee thy mother weep.   20

Sweet babe, in thy face
Holy image I can trace;
Sweet babe, once like thee,
Thy maker lay and wept for me,

Wept for me, for thee, for all,   25
When he was an infant small;
Thou his image ever see,
Heavenly face that smiles on thee –

Smiles on thee, on me, on all,
Who became an infant small: 30
Infant smiles are his own smiles;
Heaven and earth to peace beguiles.

The Divine Image

To mercy, pity, peace and love
All pray in their distress;
And to these virtues of delight
Return their thankfulness.

For mercy, pity, peace and love   5
Is God our Father dear;
And mercy, pity, peace and love
Is man, his child and care.

For mercy has a human heart,
Pity, a human face,   10
And love, the human form divine,
And peace, the human dress.

Then every man of every clime
That prays in his distress,
Prays to the human form divine –   15
Love, mercy, pity, peace.

And all must love the human form
In heathen, Turk, or Jew;
Where mercy, love and pity dwell
There God is dwelling too.   20

Holy Thursday

'Twas on a Holy Thursday, their innocent faces clean,
The children walking two and two in red and blue and green,
Grey-headed beadles walked before, with wands as white as snow,
Till into the high dome of Paul's they like Thames' waters flow.

Oh what a multitude they seemed, these flowers of London town!   5
Seated in companies they sit, with radiance all their own;
The hum of multitudes was there, but multitudes of lambs –
Thousands of little boys and girls raising their innocent hands.

Now like a mighty wind they raise to heaven the voice of song,
Or like harmonious thunderings the seats of heaven among;   10
Beneath them sit the aged men, wise guardians of the poor;
Then cherish pity, lest you drive an angel from your door.

Night

The sun descending in the west,
The evening star does shine;
The birds are silent in their nest
And I must seek for mine.
The moon like a flower   5
In heaven's high bower,
With silent delight
Sits and smiles on the night.

Farewell, green fields and happy groves,
Where flocks have took delight;   10
Where lambs have nibbled, silent moves
The feet of angels bright;
Unseen they pour blessing
And joy without ceasing
On each bud and blossom   15
And each sleeping bosom.

They look in every thoughtless nest
Where birds are covered warm,
They visit caves of every beast
To keep them all from harm.   20
If they see any weeping
That should have been sleeping,
They pour sleep on their head
And sit down by their bed.

When wolves and tigers howl for prey   25
They pitying stand and weep,
Seeking to drive their thirst away
And keep them from the sheep;
But if they rush dreadful,
The angels most heedful   30
Receive each mild spirit,
New worlds to inherit.

And there the lion's ruddy eyes
Shall flow with tears of gold,
And pitying the tender cries,   35
And walking round the fold,
Saying, 'Wrath, by his meekness,
And by his health, sickness

Is driven away
From our immortal day.   40

And now beside thee, bleating lamb,
I can lie down and sleep,
Or think on him who bore thy name,
Graze after thee and weep.
For, washed in life's river,   45
My bright mane for ever
Shall shine like the gold
As I guard o'er the fold.'

Spring

Sound the flute!
Now it's mute.
Birds delight
Day and night;
Nightingale   5
In the dale,
Lark in sky,
Merrily
Merrily, merrily, to welcome in the year.

Little boy   10
Full of joy;
Little girl
Sweet and small;
Cock does crow,
So do you;   15
Merry voice,
Infant noise –
Merrily, merrily, to welcome in the year.

Little lamb
Here I am,   20
Come and lick
My white neck!
Let me pull
Your soft wool,
Let me kiss   25
Your soft face;
Merrily, merrily, we welcome in the year.

Nurse's Song

When the voices of children are heard on the green
And laughing is heard on the hill,
My heart is at rest within my breast
And everything else is still.

'Then come home, my children, the sun is gone down   5
And the dews of night arise;
Come, come, leave off play, and let us away
Till the morning appears in the skies.'

'No, no! Let us play, for it is yet day
And we cannot go to sleep;   10
Besides, in the sky, the little birds fly
And the hills are all covered with sheep.'

'Well, well, go and play till the light fades away
And then go home to bed.'
The little ones leaped and shouted and laughed   15
And all the hills echoed.

Infant Joy

'I have no name,
I am but two days old.'
What shall I call thee?
'I happy am,
Joy is my name.'   5
Sweet joy befall thee!

Pretty joy!
Sweet joy but two days old,
Sweet joy I call thee;
Thou dost smile,   10
I sing the while,
Sweet joy befall thee!

A Dream

Once a dream did weave a shade
O'er my angel-guarded bed,
That an emmet lost its way
Where on grass methought I lay.

Troubled, wildered, and forlorn,   5
Dark, benighted, travel-worn,
Over many a tangled spray,
All heart-broke I heard her say,

'Oh my children! Do they cry?
Do they hear their father sigh?   10
Now they look abroad to see;
Now return and weep for me.'

Pitying, I dropped a tear;
But I saw a glow-worm near
Who replied, 'What wailing wight   15
Calls the watchman of the night?

I am set to light the ground
While the beetle goes his round;
Follow now the beetle's hum –
Little wanderer, hie thee home.'   20

On Another's Sorrow

Can I see another's woe
And not be in sorrow too?
Can I see another's grief
And not seek for kind relief?

Can I see a falling tear   5
And not feel my sorrow's share?
Can a father see his child
Weep, nor be with sorrow filled?

Can a mother sit and hear
An infant groan, an infant fear?   10
No, no! never can it be!
Never, never can it be!

And can He who smiles on all,
Hear the wren with sorrows small,
Hear the small bird's grief and care,   15
Hear the woes that infants bear –

And not sit beside the nest
Pouring pity in their breast?
And not sit the cradle near
Weeping tear on infant's tear?   20

And not sit both night and day
Wiping all our tears away?
Oh no! never can it be!
Never, never can it be!

He doth give his joy to all,   25
He becomes an infant small;
He becomes a man of woe,
He doth feel the sorrow too.

Think not thou canst sigh a sigh
And thy maker is not by;   30
Think not thou canst weep a tear
And thy maker is not near.

Oh! he gives to us his joy
That our grief he may destroy;
Till our grief is fled and gone   35
He doth sit by us and moan.

SONGS OF EXPERIENCE

Introduction

Hear the voice of the bard!
Who present, past and future sees;
Whose ears have heard
The Holy Word
That walked among the ancient trees   5

Calling the lapsed soul,
And weeping in the evening dew;
That might control
The starry pole,
And fallen, fallen light renew!   10

'Oh Earth, oh Earth, return!
Arise from out the dewy grass;
Night is worn,
And the morn
Rises from the slumberous mass.   15

Turn away no more!
Why wilt thou turn away?
The starry floor,
The wat'ry shore,
Is giv'n thee till the break of day.'   20

Earth's Answer

Earth raised up her head
From the darkness, dread and drear;
Her light fled,
Stony dread!
And her locks covered with grey despair.   5

'Prisoned on wat'ry shore,
Starry Jealousy does keep my den;
Cold and hoar,
Weeping o'er,
I hear the father of the ancient men.   10

Selfish father of men!
Cruel, jealous, selfish fear!
Can delight
Chained in night
The virgins of youth and morning bear?   15

Does spring hide its joy
When buds and blossoms grow?
Does the sower
Sow by night,
Or the ploughman in darkness plough?   20

Break this heavy chain
That does freeze my bones around! –
Selfish, vain,
Eternal bane!
That free love with bondage bound.'   25

The Clod and the Pebble

'Love seeketh not itself to please
Nor for itself hath any care;
But for another gives its ease
And builds a heaven in hell's despair.'

So sung a little clod of clay   5
Trodden with the cattle's feet,
But a pebble of the brook
Warbled out these metres meet:

'Love seeketh only self to please,
To bind another to its delight;   10

Joys in another's loss of ease,
And builds a hell in heaven's despite.'

Holy Thursday

Is this a holy thing to see
In a rich and fruitful land?
Babes reduced to misery,
Fed with cold and usurous hand?

Is that trembling cry a song?   5
Can it be a song of joy?
And so many children poor?
It is a land of poverty!

And their sun does never shine,
And their fields are bleak and bare,   10
And their ways are filled with thorns –
It is eternal winter there.

For where'er the sun does shine
And where'er the rain does fall,
Babe can never hunger there,   15
Nor poverty the mind appal.

The Little Girl Lost

In futurity
I prophetic see
That the earth from sleep
(Grave the sentence deep)

Shall arise and seek   5
For her maker meek,
And the desert wild
Become a garden mild.

In the southern clime,
Where the summer's prime   10
Never fades away,
Lovely Lyca lay.

Seven summers old
Lovely Lyca told;
She had wandered long   15
Hearing wild birds' song.

'Sweet sleep, come to me
Underneath this tree;
Do father, mother weep?
Where can Lyca sleep?   20

Lost in desert wild
Is your little child;
How can Lyca sleep
If her mother weep?

If her heart does ache   25
Then let Lyca wake;
If my mother sleep
Lyca shall not weep.

Frowning, frowning night,
O'er this desert bright,   30
Let thy moon arise
While I close my eyes.'

Sleeping Lyca lay
While the beasts of prey,
Come from caverns deep,   35
Viewed the maid asleep.

The kingly lion stood
And the virgin viewed,
Then he gambolled round
O'er the hallowed ground.   40

Leopards, tigers play
Round her as she lay,
While the lion old
Bowed his mane of gold

And her bosom lick,   45
And upon her neck
From his eyes of flame
Ruby tears there came;

While the lioness
Loosed her slender dress,   50
And naked they conveyed
To caves the sleeping maid.

The Little Girl Found

All the night in woe
Lyca's parents go;
Over valleys deep,
While the deserts weep.

Tired and woe-begone,   5
Hoarse with making moan,
Arm in arm seven days
They traced the desert ways.

Seven nights they sleep
Among shadows deep,   10
And dream they see their child
Starved in desert wild.

Pale through pathless ways
The fancied image strays
Famished, weeping, weak,   15
With hollow piteous shriek.

Rising from unrest,
The trembling woman pressed
With feet of weary woe;
She could no further go.   20

In his arms he bore
Her, armed with sorrow sore;
Till before their way
A couching lion lay.

Turning back was vain;   25
Soon his heavy mane
Bore them to the ground:
Then he stalked around

Smelling to his prey.
But their fears allay   30
When he licks their hands,
And silent by them stands.

They look upon his eyes
Filled with deep surprise,
And wondering behold   35
A spirit armed in gold.

On his head a crown,
On his shoulders down
Flowed his golden hair;
Gone was all their care.   40

'Follow me', he said,
'Weep not for the maid;
In my palace deep
Lyca lies asleep.'

Then they followed   45
Where the vision led,
And saw their sleeping child
Among tigers wild.

To this day they dwell
In a lonely dell;   50
Nor fear the wolvish howl,
Nor the lion's growl.

The Chimney Sweeper

A little black thing among the snow,
Crying 'weep weep' in notes of woe;
'Where are thy father and mother, say?'
'They are both gone up to the church to pray.

Because I was happy upon the heath   5
And smiled among the winter's snow,
They clothed me in the clothes of death,
And taught me to sing the notes of woe.

And because I am happy and dance and sing,
They think they have done me no injury,   10
And are gone to praise God and his priest and king,
Who make up a heaven of our misery.'

Nurse's Song

When the voices of children are heard on the green
And whisp' rings are in the dale,
The days of my youth rise fresh in my mind,
My face turns green and pale.

Then come home, my children, the sun is gone down,   5
And the dews of night arise;
Your spring and your day are wasted in play,
And your winter and night in disguise.

The Sick Rose

Oh rose, thou art sick;
The invisible worm
That flies in the night
In the howling storm

Has found out thy bed   5
Of crimson joy,
And his dark secret love
Does thy life destroy.

The Fly

Little fly,
Thy summer's play
My thoughtless hand
Has brushed away.

Am not I   5
A fly like thee?
Or art not thou
A man like me?

For I dance
And drink and sing   10
Till some blind hand
Shall brush my wing.

If thought is life
And strength and breath,
And the want   15
Of thought is death,

Then am I
A happy fly,
If I live
Or if I die.   20

The Angel

I dreamt a dream! What can it mean?
And that I was a maiden queen
Guarded by an angel mild:
Witless woe was ne'er beguiled!

And I wept both night and day,   5
And he wiped my tears away,
And I wept both day and night,
And hid from him my heart's delight.

So he took his wings and fled,
Then the morn blushed rosy red;   10
I dried my tears, and armed my fears
With ten thousand shields and spears.

Soon my angel came again:
I was armed, he came in vain –
For the time of youth was fled,   15
And grey hairs were on my head

The Tyger

Tyger, tyger, burning bright
In the forests of the night,
What immortal hand or eye
Could frame thy fearful symmetry?

In what distant deeps or skies   5
Burnt the fire of thine eyes?
On what wings dare he aspire?
What the hand dare seize the fire?

And what shoulder and what art
Could twist the sinews of thy heart?   10
And when thy heart began to beat,
What dread hand and what dread feet?

What the hammer? What the chain?
In what furnace was thy brain?
What the anvil? What dread grasp   15
Dare its deadly terrors clasp?

When the stars threw down their spears
And watered heaven with their tears,
Did he smile his work to see?
Did he who made the lamb make thee?   20

Tyger, tyger, burning bright
In the forests of the night,
What immortal hand or eye
Dare frame thy fearful symmetry?

My Pretty Rose-Tree

A flower was offered to me,
Such a flower as May never bore;
But I said, 'I've a pretty rose-tree',
And I passed the sweet flower o'er.

Then I went to my pretty rose-tree   5
To tend her by day and by night;
But my rose turned away with jealousy
And her thorns were my only delight.

Ah, Sunflower!

Ah, sunflower! weary of time,
Who countest the steps of the sun,
Seeking after that sweet golden clime
Where the traveller's journey is done;

Where the youth pined away with desire,   5
And the pale virgin shrouded in snow,
Arise from their graves and aspire
Where my sunflower wishes to go.

The Lily

The modest rose puts forth a thorn,
The humble sheep a threat'ning horn;
While the lily white shall in love delight,
Nor a thorn nor a threat stain her beauty bright.

The Garden of Love

I went to the Garden of Love
And saw what I never had seen:
A chapel was built in the midst
Where I used to play on the green.

And the gates of this chapel were shut,   5
And 'Thou shalt not' writ over the door;

So I turned to the Garden of Love
That so many sweet flowers bore,

And I saw it was filled with graves
And tombstones where flowers should be;   10
And priests in black gowns were walking their rounds,
And binding with briars my joys and desires.

The Little Vagabond

Dear mother, dear mother, the church is cold
But the alehouse is healthy and pleasant and warm;
Besides I can tell where I am used well –
Such usage in heaven will never do well.

But if at the church they would give us some ale,   5
And a pleasant fire our souls to regale,
We'd sing and we'd pray all the livelong day,
Nor ever once wish from the church to stray.

Then the parson might preach and drink and sing,
And we'd be as happy as birds in the spring;   10
And modest Dame Lurch, who is always at church,
Would not have bandy children nor fasting nor birch.

And God, like a father rejoicing to see
His children as pleasant and happy as he,
Would have no more quarrel with the devil or the barrel,   15
But kiss him and give him both drink and apparel.

London

I wander through each chartered street
Near where the chartered Thames does flow,
And mark in every face I meet
Marks of weakness, marks of woe.

In every cry of every man,   5
In every infant's cry of fear,
In every voice, in every ban,
The mind-forged manacles I hear.

How the chimney-sweeper's cry
Every black'ning church appals,   10
And the hapless soldier's sigh
Runs in blood down palace walls.

But most through midnight streets I hear
How the youthful harlot's curse
Blasts the new born infant's tear,   15
And blights with plagues the marriage hearse.

The Human Abstract

Pity would be no more
If we did not make somebody poor;
And mercy no more could be,
If all were as happy as we.

And mutual fear brings peace   5
Till the selfish loves increase;
Then Cruelty knits a snare
And spreads his baits with care.

He sits down with holy fears
And waters the ground with tears;   10
Then humility takes its root
Underneath his foot.

Soon spreads the dismal shade
Of mystery over his head,
And the caterpillar and fly   15
Feed on the mystery.

And it bears the fruit of deceit,
Ruddy and sweet to eat;
And the raven his nest has made
In its thickest shade.   20

The gods of the earth and sea
Sought through nature to find this tree,
But their search was all in vain –
There grows one in the human brain.

Infant Sorrow

My mother groaned, my father wept!
Into the dangerous world I leapt:
Helpless, naked, piping loud
Like a fiend hid in a cloud.

Struggling in my father's hands,   5
Striving against my swaddling bands,

Bound and weary I thought best
To sulk upon my mother's breast.

A Poison Tree

I was angry with my friend;
I told my wrath, my wrath did end.
I was angry with my foe;
I told it not, my wrath did grow.

And I watered it in fears,   5
Night and morning with my tears;
And I sunned it with smiles,
And with soft deceitful wiles.

And it grew both day and night
Till it bore an apple bright;   10
And my foe beheld it shine,
And he knew that it was mine.

And into my garden stole
When the night had veiled the pole –
In the morning glad I see   15
My foe outstretched beneath the tree.

A Little Boy Lost

'Nought loves another as itself,
Nor venerates another so,
Nor is it possible to thought
A greater than itself to know.

And, father, how can I love you   5
Or any of my brothers more?
I love you like the little bird
That picks up crumbs around the door.'

The priest sat by and heard the child,
In trembling zeal he seized his hair;   10
He led him by his little coat
And all admired the priestly care.

And standing on the altar high,
'Lo, what a fiend is here!' said he,
'One who sets reason up for judge   15
Of our most holy mystery.'

The weeping child could not be heard,
The weeping parents wept in vain;
They stripped him to his little shirt
And bound him in an iron chain,   20

And burned him in a holy place
Where many had been burned before.
The weeping parents wept in vain –
Are such things done on Albion's shore?

A Little Girl Lost

Children of the future age
Reading this indignant page,
Know that in a former time
Love! sweet Love! was thought a crime.

In the age of gold,   5
Free from winter's cold,
Youth and maiden bright
To the holy light,
Naked in the sunny beams delight.

Once a youthful pair   10
Filled with softest care
Met in garden bright
Where the holy light
Had just removed the curtains of the night.

There in rising day   15
On the grass they play;
Parents were afar,
Strangers came not near,
And the maiden soon forgot her fear.

Tired with kisses sweet,   20
They agree to meet
When the silent sleep
Waves o'er heavens deep,
And the weary tired wanderers weep.

To her father white   25
Came the maiden bright,
But his loving look,
Like the holy book
All her tender limbs with terror shook.

'Ona, pale and weak,　　　　　　　　　　　　　　30
To thy father speak! –
Oh, the trembling fear!
Oh, the dismal care
That shakes the blossoms of my hoary hair!'

To Tirzah

Whate'er is born of mortal birth
Must be consumed with the earth
To rise from generation free;
Then what have I to do with thee?

The sexes sprung from shame and pride –　　　　5
Blowed in the morn, in evening died;
But mercy changed death into sleep –
The sexes rose to work and weep.

Thou mother of my mortal part,
With cruelty didst mould my heart　　　　　　　10
And with false self-deceiving tears
Didst bind my nostrils, eyes and ears;

Didst close my tongue in senseless clay
And me to mortal life betray:
The death of Jesus set me free –　　　　　　　15
Then what have I to do with thee?

　　　　　　　　　　　　　　　　　It is raised
　　　　　　　　　　　　　　　　a spiritual body

The Schoolboy

I love to rise in a summer morn
When the birds sing on every tree;
The distant huntsman winds his horn,
And the skylark sings with me –
Oh, what sweet company!　　　　　　　　　　5

But to go to school in a summer morn,
Oh, it drives all joy away;
Under a cruel eye outworn,
The little ones spend the day
In sighing and dismay.　　　　　　　　　　　10

Ah! then at times I drooping sit
And spend many an anxious hour;
Nor in my book can I take delight,

Nor sit in learning's bower,
Worn through with the dreary shower.   15

How can the bird that is born for joy
Sit in a cage and sing?
How can a child, when fears annoy,
But droop his tender wing
And forget his youthful spring?   20

Oh, father and mother, if buds are nipped
And blossoms blown away,
And if the tender plants are stripped
Of their joy in the springing day
By sorrow and care's dismay,   25

How shall the summer arise in joy
Or the summer fruits appear?
Or how shall we gather what griefs destroy,
Or bless the mellowing year
When the blasts of winter appear?   30

The Voice of the Ancient Bard

Youth of delight, come hither
And see the opening morn –
Image of truth new-born;
Doubt is fled, and clouds of reason,
Dark disputes and artful teasing.   5
Folly is an endless maze,
Tangled roots perplex her ways –
How many have fallen there!
They stumble all night over bones of the dead,
And feel they know not what but care,   10
And wish to lead others, when they should be led.

A Divine Image

Cruelty has a human heart
And jealousy a human face;
Terror the human form divine,
And secrecy the human dress.

The human dress is forged iron,   5
The human form a fiery forge,
The human face a furnace sealed,
The human heart its hungry gorge.

William Wordsworth
(1770–1850)

Lines written a few miles above Tintern Abbey, on revisiting the banks of the Wye during a tour, 13 July 1798

Five years have passed; five summers, with the length
Of five long winters! And again I hear
These waters, rolling from their mountain springs
With a sweet inland murmur. Once again
Do I behold these steep and lofty cliffs,   5
Which on a wild secluded scene impress
Thoughts of more deep seclusion, and connect
The landscape with the quiet of the sky.
The day is come when I again repose
Here, under this dark sycamore, and view   10
These plots of cottage-ground, these orchard-tufts,
Which, at this season, with their unripe fruits,
Among the woods and copses lose themselves,
Nor, with their green and simple hue, disturb
The wild green landscape. Once again I see   15
These hedgerows – hardly hedgerows, little lines
Of sportive wood run wild; these pastoral farms
Green to the very door; and wreaths of smoke
Sent up in silence from among the trees,
With some uncertain notice, as might seem,   20
Of vagrant dwellers in the houseless woods,
Or of some hermit's cave, where by his fire
The hermit sits alone.
                            Though absent long,
These forms of beauty have not been to me
As is a landscape to a blind man's eye;   25
But oft, in lonely rooms, and mid the din
Of towns and cities, I have owed to them,
In hours of weariness, sensations sweet,
Felt in the blood, and felt along the heart,
And passing even into my purer mind   30
With tranquil restoration; feelings too
Of unremembered pleasure – such, perhaps,

As may have had no trivial influence
On that best portion of a good man's life,
His little, nameless, unremembered acts   35
Of kindness and of love. Nor less, I trust,
To them I may have owed another gift,
Of aspect more sublime; that blessed mood
In which the burden of the mystery,
In which the heavy and the weary weight   40
Of all this unintelligible world
Is lightened – that serene and blessed mood
In which the affections gently lead us on
Until the breath of this corporeal frame
And even the motion of our human blood   45
Almost suspended, we are laid asleep
In body, and become a living soul,
While with an eye made quiet by the power
Of harmony, and the deep power of joy,
We see into the life of things.
                              If this   50
Be but a vain belief – yet oh, how oft
In darkness, and amid the many shapes
Of joyless daylight, when the fretful stir
Unprofitable, and the fever of the world,
Have hung upon the beatings of my heart,   55
How oft, in spirit, have I turned to thee,
Oh sylvan Wye! Thou wanderer through the woods,
How often has my spirit turned to thee!
        And now, with gleams of half-extinguished thought,
With many recognitions dim and faint   60
And somewhat of a sad perplexity,
The picture of the mind revives again;
While here I stand, not only with the sense
Of present pleasure, but with pleasing thoughts
That in this moment there is life and food   65
For future years. And so I dare to hope,
Though changed, no doubt, from what I was when first
I came among these hills, when like a roe
I bounded o'er the mountains by the sides
Of the deep rivers and the lonely streams   70
Wherever nature led, more like a man
Flying from something that he dreads than one
Who sought the thing he loved. For nature then
(The coarser pleasures of my boyish days
And their glad animal movements all gone by)   75
To me was all in all.
                      I cannot paint
What then I was The sounding cataract
Haunted me like a passion; the tall rock,

The mountain, and the deep and gloomy wood,
Their colours and their forms, were then to me   80
An appetite, a feeling and a love
That had no need of a remoter charm
By thought supplied, or any interest
Unborrowed from the eye. That time is past,
And all its aching joys are now no more,   85
And all its dizzy raptures. Not for this
Faint I, nor mourn, nor murmur; other gifts
Have followed – for such loss, I would believe,
Abundant recompense. For I have learned
To look on nature not as in the hour   90
Of thoughtless youth, but hearing oftentimes
The still, sad music of humanity,
Not harsh nor grating, though of ample power
To chasten and subdue. And I have felt
A presence that disturbs me with the joy   95
Of elevated thoughts, a sense sublime
Of something far more deeply interfused,
Whose dwelling is the light of setting suns,
And the round ocean, and the living air,
And the blue sky, and in the mind of man –   100
A motion and a spirit that impels
All thinking things, all objects of all thought,
And rolls through all things. Therefore am I still
A lover of the meadows and the woods
And mountains, and of all that we behold   105
From this green earth, of all the mighty world
Of eye and ear (both what they half-create
And what perceive) – well-pleased to recognize
In nature and the language of the sense,
The anchor of my purest thoughts, the nurse,   110
The guide, the guardian of my heart, and soul
Of all my moral being.
      Nor, perchance,
If I were not thus taught, should I the more
Suffer my genial spirits to decay;
For thou art with me, here, upon the banks   115
Of this fair river – thou, my dearest friend,
My dear, dear friend, and in thy voice I catch
The language of my former heart, and read
My former pleasures in the shooting lights
Of thy wild eyes. Oh, yet a little while   120
May I behold in thee what I was once,
My dear, dear sister! And this prayer I make,
Knowing that Nature never did betray
The heart that loved her; 'tis her privilege,
Through all the years of this our life, to lead   125

From joy to joy, for she can so inform
The mind that is within us, so impress
With quietness and beauty, and so feed
With lofty thoughts, that neither evil tongues,
Rash judgements, nor the sneers of selfish men,   130
Nor greetings where no kindness is, nor all
The dreary intercourse of daily life,
Shall e'er prevail against us, or disturb
Our cheerful faith that all which we behold
Is full of blessings. Therefore let the moon   135
Shine on thee in thy solitary walk,
And let the misty mountain-winds be free
To blow against thee. And in after-years,
When these wild ecstasies shall be matured
Into a sober pleasure, when thy mind   140
Shall be a mansion for all lovely forms,
Thy memory be as a dwelling-place
For all sweet sounds and harmonies – oh then
If solitude, or fear, or pain, or grief
Should be thy portion, with what healing thoughts   145
Of tender joy wilt thou remember me,
And these my exhortations! Nor perchance,
If I should be where I no more can hear
Thy voice, nor catch from thy wild eyes these gleams
Of past existence, wilt thou then forget   150
That on the banks of this delightful stream
We stood together; and that I, so long
A worshipper of nature, hither came
Unwearied in that service – rather say
With warmer love, oh with far deeper zeal   155
Of holier love! Nor wilt thou then forget
That, after many wanderings, many years
Of absence, these steep woods and lofty cliffs
And this green pastoral landscape, were to me
More dear, both for themselves, and for thy sake.   160

The Two-Part Prelude (Part I)

                    Was it for this
That one, the fairest of all rivers, loved
To blend his murmurs with my nurse's song,
And from his alder shades and rocky falls,
And from his fords and shallows, sent a voice   5
That flowed along my dreams? For this didst thou,
Oh Derwent, travelling over the green plains
Near my 'sweet birthplace', didst thou, beauteous stream,
Make ceaseless music through the night and day,

Which with its steady cadence tempering   10
Our human waywardness, composed my thoughts
To more than infant softness, giving me,
Among the fretful dwellings of mankind,
A knowledge, a dim earnest of the calm
Which nature breathes among the fields and groves?   15
  Beloved Derwent, fairest of all streams,
Was it for this that I, a four years' child,
A naked boy, among thy silent pools,
Made one long bathing of a summer's day,
Basked in the sun, or plunged into thy streams   20
Alternate all a summer's day, or coursed
Over the sandy fields, and dashed the flowers
Of yellow grunsel; or, when crag and hill,
The woods, and distant Skiddaw's lofty height
Were bronzed with a deep radiance, stood alone,   25
A naked savage in the thunder shower?
  And afterwards, 'twas in a later day,
Though early, when upon the mountain-slope
The frost and breath of frosty wind had snapped
The last autumnal crocus, 'twas my joy   30
To wander half the night among the cliffs
And the smooth hollows where the woodcocks ran
Along the moonlight turf. In thought and wish
That time, my shoulder all with springes hung,
I was a fell destroyer. Gentle powers   35
Who give us happiness and call it peace,
When scudding on from snare to snare I plied
My anxious visitation – hurrying on,
Still hurrying, hurrying onward – how my heart
Panted among the scattered yew-trees and the crags   40
That looked upon me, how my bosom beat
With expectation! Sometimes strong desire,
Resistless, overpowered me, and the bird
Which was the captive of another's toils
Became my prey; and when the deed was done   45
I heard among the solitary hills
Low breathings coming after me, and sounds
Of undistinguishable motion, steps
Almost as silent as the turf they trod.
  Nor less in springtime, when on southern banks   50
The shining sun had from his knot of leaves
Decoyed the primrose flower, and when the vales
And woods were warm, was I a rover then
In the high places, on the lonesome peaks
Among the mountains and the winds. Though mean   55
And though inglorious were my views, the end
Was not ignoble. Oh, when I have hung

Above the raven's nest, by knots of grass
Or half-inch fissures in the slipp'ry rock
But ill sustained, and almost (as it seemed)   60
Suspended by the blast which blew amain,
Shouldering the naked crag – oh, at that time,
While on the perilous ridge I hung alone,
With what strange utterance did the loud dry wind
Blow through my ears! The sky seemed not a sky   65
Of earth, and with what motion moved the clouds!
    The mind of man is fashioned and built up
Even as a strain of music; I believe
That there are spirits which, when they would form
A favoured being, from his very dawn   70
Of infancy do open out the clouds
As at the touch of lightning, seeking him
With gentle visitation – quiet powers,
Retired and seldom recognized, yet kind
And to the very meanest not unknown.   75
With me, though rarely, in my early days,
They communed; others too there are who use,
Yet haply aiming at the self-same end,
Severer interventions, ministry
More palpable – and of their school was I.   80
    They guided me. One evening, led by them,
I went alone into a shepherd's boat,
A skiff that to a willow-tree was tied
Within a rocky cave, its usual home.
The moon was up, the lake was shining clear   85
Among the hoary mountains; from the shore
I pushed, and struck the oars, and struck again
In cadence, and my little boat moved on
Just like a man who walks with stately step
Though bent on speed. It was an act of stealth   90
And troubled pleasure; not without the voice
Of mountain-echoes did my boat move on,
Leaving behind her still on either side
Small circles glittering idly in the moon
Until they melted all into one track   95
Of sparkling light. A rocky steep uprose
Above the cavern of the willow-tree,
And now, as suited one who proudly rowed
With his best skill, I fixed a steady view
Upon the top of that same craggy ridge,   100
The bound of the horizon, for behind
Was nothing but the stars and the grey sky
She was an elfin pinnace; twenty times
I dipped my oars into the silent lake,
And, as I rose upon the stroke, my boat   105

Went heaving through the water like a swan –
When, from behind that rocky steep (till then
The bound of the horizon), a huge cliff,
As if with voluntary power instinct,
Upreared its head. I struck and struck again,   110
And, growing still in stature, the huge cliff
Rose up between me and the stars, and still,
With measured motion, like a living thing
Strode after me. With trembling hands I turned,
And through the silent water stole my way   115
Back to the cavern of the willow-tree.
There in her mooring-place I left my bark,
And through the meadows homeward went with grave
And serious thoughts; and after I had seen
That spectacle, for many days my brain   120
Worked with a dim and undetermined sense
Of unknown modes of being. In my thoughts
There was a darkness – call it solitude
Or blank desertion; no familiar shapes
Of hourly objects, images of trees,   125
Of sea or sky, no colours of green fields,
But huge and mighty forms that do not live
Like living men moved slowly through my mind
By day, and were the trouble of my dreams.
    Ah, not in vain, ye beings of the hills,   130
And ye that walk the woods and open heaths
By moon or starlight, thus from my first dawn
Of childhood did ye love to intertwine
The passions that build up our human soul,
Not with the mean and vulgar works of man,   135
But with high objects, with eternal things,
With life and nature, purifying thus
The elements of feeling and of thought,
And sanctifying by such discipline
Both pain and fear, until we recognize   140
A grandeur in the beatings of the heart.
    Nor was this fellowship vouchsafed to me
With stinted kindness. In November days,
When vapours rolling down the valleys made
A lonely scene more lonesome, among woods   145
At noon, and mid the calm of summer nights
When by the margin of the trembling lake
Beneath the gloomy hills I homeward went
In solitude, such intercourse was mine.
    And in the frosty season, when the sun   150
Was set, and visible for many a mile,
The cottage windows through the twilight blazed,
I heeded not the summons; clear and loud

The village clock tolled six; I wheeled about,
Proud and exulting like an untired horse   155
That cares not for its home. All shod with steel
We hissed along the polished ice in games
Confederate, imitative of the chase
And woodland pleasures – the resounding horn,
The pack loud bellowing, and the hunted hare.   160
So through the darkness and the cold we flew,
And not a voice was idle. With the din,
Meanwhile, the precipices rang aloud,
The leafless trees and every icy crag
Tinkled like iron, while the distant hills   165
Into the tumult sent an alien sound
Of melancholy not unnoticed – while the stars
Eastward were sparkling clear, and in the west
The orange sky of evening died away.
  Not seldom from the uproar I retired   170
Into a silent bay, or sportively
Glanced sideway, leaving the tumultuous throng,
To cut across the shadow of a star
That gleamed upon the ice. And oftentimes,
When we had given our bodies to the wind,   175
And all the shadowy banks on either side
Came sweeping through the darkness, spinning still
The rapid line of motion – then at once
Have I, reclining back upon my heels,
Stopped short: yet still the solitary cliffs   180
Wheeled by me, even as if the earth had rolled
With visible motion her diurnal round;
Behind me did they stretch in solemn train
Feebler and feebler, and I stood and watched
Till all was tranquil as a summer sea.   185
  Ye powers of earth, ye genii of the springs!
And ye that have your voices in the clouds
And ye that are familiars of the lakes
And of the standing pools, I may not think
A vulgar hope was yours when ye employed   190
Such ministry – when ye through many a year
Thus by the agency of boyish sports
On caves and trees, upon the woods and hills,
Impressed upon all forms the characters
Of danger or desire, and thus did make   195
The surface of the universal earth
With meanings of delight, of hope and fear,
Work like a sea.
                    Not uselessly employed,
I might pursue this theme through every change
Of exercise and sport to which the year   200

Did summon us in its delightful round.
We were a noisy crew; the sun in heaven
Beheld not vales more beautiful than ours,
Nor saw a race in happiness and joy
More worthy of the fields where they were sown.   205
I would record with no reluctant voice
Our home amusements by the warm peat-fire
At evening, when with pencil and with slate,
In square divisions parcelled out, and all
With crosses and with cyphers scribbled o'er,   210
We schemed and puzzled, head opposed to head,
In strife too humble to be named in verse;
Or round the naked table, snow-white deal,
Cherry or maple, sat in close array,
And to the combat, loo or whist, led on   215
A thick-ribbed army – not (as in the world)
Discarded and ungratefully thrown by
Even for the very service they had wrought,
But husbanded through many a long campaign.
Oh with what echoes on the board they fell!   220
Ironic diamonds, hearts of sable hue,
Queens gleaming through their splendour's last decay,
Knaves wrapped in one assimilating gloom,
And kings indignant at the shame incurred
By royal visages. Meanwhile abroad   225
The heavy rain was falling, or the frost
Raged bitterly with keen and silent tooth,
Or, interrupting the impassioned game,
Oft from the neighbouring lake the splitting ice,
While it sank down towards the water, sent   230
Among the meadows and the hills its long
And frequent yellings, imitative some
Of wolves that howl along the Bothnic main.
     Nor with less willing heart would I rehearse
The woods of autumn and their hidden bowers   235
With milk-white clusters hung, the rod and line
(True symbol of the foolishness of hope)
Which with its strong enchantment led me on
By rocks and pools where never summer star
Impressed its shadow, to forlorn cascades   240
Among the windings of the mountain-brooks;
The kite, in sultry calms from some high hill
Sent up, ascending thence till it was lost
Among the fleecy clouds, in gusty days
Launched from the lower grounds, and suddenly   245
Dashed headlong – and rejected by the storm.
All these and more with rival claims demand
Grateful acknowledgement. It were a song

Venial, and such as if I rightly judge
I might protract unblamed, but I perceive   250
That much is overlooked, and we should ill
Attain our object if from delicate fears
Of breaking in upon the unity
Of this my argument I should omit
To speak of such effects as cannot here   255
By regularly classed, yet tend no less
To the same point, the growth of mental power
And love of nature's works.
                             Ere I had seen
Eight summers – and 'twas in the very week
When I was first entrusted to thy vale,   260
Beloved Hawkshead! – when thy paths, thy shores
And brooks, were like a dream of novelty
To my half-infant mind, I chanced to cross
One of those open fields which, shaped like ears,
Make green peninsulas on Esthwaite's Lake.   265
Twilight was coming on, yet through the gloom
I saw distinctly on the opposite shore,
Beneath a tree and close by the lakeside,
A heap of garments, as if left by one
Who there was bathing. Half an hour I watched   270
And no one owned them; meanwhile the calm lake
Grew dark with all the shadows on its breast,
And now and then a leaping fish disturbed
The breathless stillness. The succeeding day
There came a company, and in their boat   275
Sounded with iron hooks and with long poles.
At length the dead man, mid that beauteous scene
Of trees and hills and water, bolt upright
Rose with his ghastly face. I might advert
To numerous accidents in flood or field,   280
Quarry or moor, or mid the winter snows,
Distresses and disasters, tragic facts
Of rural history that impressed my mind
With images to which, in following years,
Far other feelings were attached, with forms   285
That yet exist with independent life,
And, like their archetypes, know no decay.
    There are in our existence spots of time
Which with distinct pre-eminence retain
A fructifying virtue, whence, depressed   290
By trivial occupations and the round
Of ordinary intercourse, our minds
(Especially the imaginative power)
Are nourished, and invisibly repaired.
Such moments chiefly seem to have their date   295

In our first childhood.
                 I remember well
('Tis of an early season that I speak,
The twilight of rememberable life)
While I was yet an urchin, one who scarce
Could hold a bridle, with ambitious hopes   300
I mounted, and we rode towards the hills.
We were a pair of horsemen: honest James
Was with me, my encourager and guide.
We had not travelled long ere some mischance
Disjoined me from my comrade and, through fear   305
Dismounting, down the rough and stony moor
I led my horse, and, stumbling on, at length
Came to a bottom where in former times
A man, the murderer of his wife, was hung
In irons; mouldered was the gibbet-mast,   310
The bones were gone, the iron and the wood,
Only a long green ridge of turf remained
Whose shape was like a grave. I left the spot
And, reascending the bare slope, I saw
A naked pool that lay beneath the hills,   315
The beacon on the summit, and, more near,
A girl who bore a pitcher on her head
And seemed with difficult steps to force her way
Against the blowing wind. It was in truth
An ordinary sight, but I should need   320
Colours and words that are unknown to man
To paint the visionary dreariness
Which, while I looked all round for my lost guide,
Did at that time invest the naked pool,
The beacon on the lonely eminence,   325
The woman and her garments vexed and tossed
By the strong wind.
              Nor less I recollect,
Long after, though my childhood had not ceased,
Another scene which left a kindred power
Implanted in my mind. One Christmas-time,   330
The day before the holidays began,
Feverish and tired and restless, I went forth
Into the fields, impatient for the sight
Of those three horses which should bear us home,
My brothers and myself. There was a crag,   335
An eminence which from the meeting-point
Of two highways ascending, overlooked
At least a long half-mile of those two roads,
By each of which the expected steeds might come,
The choice uncertain. Thither I repaired   340
Up to the highest summit. 'Twas a day

Stormy, and rough, and wild, and on the grass
I sat, half-sheltered by a naked wall;
Upon my right hand was a single sheep,
A whistling hawthorn on my left, and there,   345
Those two companions at my side, I watched,
With eyes intensely straining, as the mist
Gave intermitting prospects of the wood
And plain beneath. Ere I to school returned
That dreary time, ere I had been ten days   350
A dweller in my father's house, he died,
And I and my two brothers, orphans then,
Followed his body to the grave. The event,
With all the sorrow which it brought, appeared
A chastisement, and when I called to mind   355
That day so lately past, when from the crag
I looked in such anxiety of hope,
With trite reflections of morality,
Yet with the deepest passion, I bowed low
To God, who thus corrected my desires.   360
And afterwards the wind and sleety rain
And all the business of the elements,
The single sheep, and the one blasted tree,
And the bleak music of that old stone wall,
The noise of wood and water, and the mist   365
Which on the line of each of those two roads
Advanced in such indisputable shapes –
All these were spectacles and sounds to which
I often would repair, and thence would drink
As at a fountain. And I do not doubt   370
That in this later time, when storm and rain
Beat on my roof at midnight, or by day
When I am in the woods, unknown to me
The workings of my spirit thence are brought.
    Nor, sedulous as I have been to trace   375
How nature by collateral interest
And by extrinsic passion peopled first
My mind with forms or beautiful or grand
And made me love them, may I well forget
How other pleasures have been mine, and joys   380
Of subtler origin – how I have felt,
Not seldom, even in that tempestuous time,
Those hallowed and pure motions of the sense
Which seem in their simplicity to own
An intellectual charm, that calm delight   385
Which, if I err not, surely must belong
To those first-born affinities that fit
Our new existence to existing things,
And in our dawn of being constitute

The bond of union betwixt life and joy.   390
   Yes, I remember when the changeful earth
And twice five seasons on my mind had stamped
The faces of the moving year; even then,
A child, I held unconscious intercourse
With the eternal beauty, drinking in   395
A pure organic pleasure from the lines
Of curling mist, or from the level plain
Of waters coloured by the steady clouds.
   The sands of Westmorland, the creeks and bays
Of Cumbria's rocky limits, they can tell   400
How when the sea threw off his evening shade
And to the shepherd's hut beneath the crags
Did send sweet notice of the rising moon,
How I have stood, to images like these
A stranger, linking with the spectacle   405
No body of associated forms
And bringing with me no peculiar sense
Of quietness or peace – yet I have stood,
Even while my eye has moved o'er three long leagues
Of shining water, gathering, as it seemed,   410
Through the wide surface of that field of light
New pleasure like a bee among the flowers.
   Thus often in those fits of vulgar joy
Which through all seasons on a child's pursuits
Are prompt attendants, mid that giddy bliss   415
Which like a tempest works along the blood
And is forgotten – even then I felt
Gleams like the flashing of a shield. The earth
And common face of nature spake to me
Rememberable things – sometimes, 'tis true,   420
By quaint associations, yet not vain
Nor profitless if haply they impressed
Collateral objects and appearances,
Albeit lifeless then, and doomed to sleep
Until maturer seasons called them forth   425
To impregnate and to elevate the mind.
And if the vulgar joy by its own weight
Wearied itself out of the memory,
The scenes which were a witness of that joy
Remained in their substantial lineaments   430
Depicted on the brain, and to the eye
Were visible, a daily sight. And thus,
By the impressive agency of fear,
By pleasure, and repeated happiness,
So frequently repeated, and by force   435
Of obscure feelings representative
Of joys that were forgotten, these same scenes

So beauteous and majestic in themselves,
Though yet the day was distant, did at length
Become habitually dear, and all   440
Their hues and forms were by invisible links
Allied to the affections.
                              I began
My story early, feeling, as I fear,
The weakness of a human love for days
Disowned by memory, ere the birth of spring   445
Planting my snowdrops among winter snows.
Nor will it seem to thee, my friend, so prompt
In sympathy, that I have lengthened out
With fond and feeble tongue a tedious tale.
Meanwhile my hope has been that I might fetch   450
Reproaches from my former years, whose power
May spur me on, in manhood now mature,
To honourable toil. Yet should it be
That this is but an impotent desire,
That I by such enquiry am not taught   455
To understand myself, nor thou to know
With better knowledge how the heart was framed
Of him thou lovest, need I dread from thee
Harsh judgements if I am so loath to quit
Those recollected hours that have the charm   460
Of visionary things, and lovely forms
And sweet sensations that throw back our life
And make our infancy a visible scene
On which the sun is shining?

Strange fits of passion I have known

Strange fits of passion I have known,
And I will dare to tell,
But in the lover's ear alone,
What once to me befell.

When she I loved was strong and gay   5
And like a rose in June,
I to her cottage bent my way
Beneath the evening moon.

Upon the moon I fixed my eye,
All over the wide lea;   10
My horse trudged on, and we drew nigh
Those paths so dear to me.

And now we reached the orchard-plot,
And as we climbed the hill,

Towards the roof of Lucy's cot   15
The moon descended still.

In one of those sweet dreams I slept,
Kind nature's gentlest boon!
And all the while my eyes I kept
On the descending moon.   20

My horse moved on; hoof after hoof
He raised and never stopped:
When down behind the cottage roof
At once the planet dropped.

What fond and wayward thoughts will slide   25
Into a lover's head;
'Oh mercy!' to myself I cried,
'If Lucy should be dead!'

Song

She dwelt among th' untrodden ways
   Beside the springs of Dove,
A maid whom there were none to praise
   And very few to love.

A violet by a mossy stone   5
   Half-hidden from the eye,
Fair as a star when only one
   Is shining in the sky!

She *lived* unknown, and few could know
   When Lucy ceased to be;   10
But she is in her grave, and oh!
   The difference to me.

A slumber did my spirit seal

A slumber did my spirit seal,
   I had no human fears;
She seemed a thing that could not feel
   The touch of earthly years.

No motion has she now, no force;   5
   She neither hears nor sees;
Rolled round in earth's diurnal course
   With rocks and stones and trees!

Three years she grew in sun and shower

Three years she grew in sun and shower,
Then Nature said, 'A lovelier flower
On earth was never sown;
This child I to myself will take,
She shall be mine, and I will make   5
A lady of my own.

Myself will to my darling be
Both law and impulse, and with me
The girl in rock and plain,
In earth and heaven, in glade and bower,   10
Shall feel an overseeing power
To kindle or restrain.

She shall be sportive as the fawn
That wild with glee across the lawn
Or up the mountain springs,   15
And hers shall be the breathing balm
And hers the silence and the calm
Of mute insensate things.

The floating clouds their state shall lend
To her, for her the willow bend,   20
Nor shall she fail to see
Even in the motions of the storm
A beauty that shall mould her form
By silent sympathy.

The stars of midnight shall be dear   25
To her, and she shall lean her ear
In many a secret place
Where rivulets dance their wayward round,
And beauty born of murmuring sound
Shall pass into her face.   30

And vital feelings of delight
Shall rear her form to stately height,
Her virgin bosom swell,
Such thoughts to Lucy I will give
While she and I together live   35
Here in this happy dell.'

Thus Nature spake – the work was done
How soon my Lucy's race was run!
She died and left to me

This heath, this calm and quiet scene,   40
The memory of what has been,
And never more will be.

I travelled among unknown men

I travelled among unknown men
    In lands beyond the sea;
Nor, England, did I know till then
    What love I bore to thee.

'Tis passed, that melancholy dream!   5
    Nor will I quit thy shore
A second time, for still I seem
    To love thee more and more.

Among thy mountains did I feel
    The joy of my desire;   10
And she I cherished turned her wheel
    Beside an English fire.

Thy mornings showed, thy nights concealed
    The bowers where Lucy played;
And thine is, too, the last green field   15
    Which Lucy's eyes surveyed!

Composed upon Westminster Bridge,
3 September 1802

Earth has not any thing to show more fair:
Dull would he be of soul who could pass by
A sight so touching in its majesty.
This city now doth like a garment wear
The beauty of the morning – silent, bare,   5
Ships, towers, domes, theatres, and temples lie
Open unto the fields, and to the sky,
All bright and glittering in the smokeless air.
Never did sun more beautifully steep
In his first splendour valley, rock, or hill;   10
Ne'er saw I, never felt, a calm so deep.
The river glideth at his own sweet will –
Dear God! the very houses seem asleep;
And all that mighty heart is lying still.

Ode. Intimations of Immortality from Recollections of Early Childhood

Paulò majora canamus.[1]

There was a time when meadow, grove, and stream,
The earth, and every common sight,
    To me did seem
    Apparelled in celestial light,
The glory and the freshness of a dream.   5
It is not now as it has been of yore;
    Turn wheresoe'er I may
      By night or day
The things which I have seen I now can see no more.

    The rainbow comes and goes   10
    And lovely is the rose,
    The moon doth with delight
  Look round her when the heavens are bare;
    Waters on a starry night
    Are beautiful and fair;   15
  The sunshine is a glorious birth;
  But yet I know, where'er I go,
That there hath passed away a glory from the earth.

Now while the birds thus sing a joyous song,
    And while the young lambs bound   20
    As to the tabor's sound,
To me alone there came a thought of grief;
A timely utterance gave that thought relief
    And I again am strong.
The cataracts blow their trumpets from the steep –   25
No more shall grief of mine the season wrong;
I hear the echoes through the mountains throng,
The winds come to me from the fields of sleep
    And all the earth is gay;
      Land and sea   30
  Give themselves up to jollity,
    And with the heart of May
Doth every beast keep holiday.
    Thou child of joy
Shout round me, let me hear thy shouts, thou happy
    shepherd-boy!   35

  Ye blessed creatures, I have heard the call
Ye to each other make; I see

[1] 'Let us sing of somewhat more exalted things' (Virgil, *Eclogue* iv 1).

The heavens laugh with you in your jubilee;
  My heart is at your festival,
    My head hath its coronal –   40
The fullness of your bliss, I feel, I feel it all.
    Oh evil day! if I were sullen
    While the earth herself is adorning
      This sweet May morning,
    And the children are pulling   45
      On every side
    In a thousand valleys far and wide
    Fresh flowers, while the sun shines warm
And the babe leaps up on his mother's arm –
    I hear, I hear, with joy I hear!   50
    But there's a tree, of many one,
A single field which I have looked upon,
Both of them speak of something that is gone;
    The pansy at my feet
    Doth the same tale repeat: 55
Whither is fled the visionary gleam?
Where is it now, the glory and the dream?

Our birth is but a sleep and a forgetting.
The soul that rises with us, our life's star,
    Hath had elsewhere its setting   60
      And cometh from afar.
    Not in entire forgetfulness,
    And not in utter nakedness,
But trailing clouds of glory do we come
    From God, who is our home.   65
Heaven lies about us in our infancy!
Shades of the prison-house begin to close
    Upon the growing boy,
But he beholds the light and whence it flows,
    He sees it in his joy;   70
The youth who daily farther from the east
  Must travel, still is nature's priest,
    And by the vision splendid
    Is on his way attended:
At length the man perceives it die away   75
And fade into the light of common day.

Earth fills her lap with pleasures of her own;
Yearnings she hath in her own natural kind,
And even with something of a mother's mind
    And no unworthy aim,   80
  The homely nurse doth all she can
To make her foster-child, her inmate man,
  Forget the glories he hath known
And that imperial palace whence he came.

Behold the child among his new-born blisses,   85
A four years' darling of a pygmy size!
See where mid work of his own hand he lies,
Fretted by sallies of his mother's kisses
With light upon him from his father's eyes!
See at his feet some little plan or chart,   90
Some fragment from his dream of human life
Shaped by himself with newly-learned art –
    A wedding or a festival,
    A mourning or a funeral;
      And this hath now his heart,   95
    And unto this he frames his song.
      Then will he fit his tongue
To dialogues of business, love, or strife;
    But it will not be long
    Ere this be thrown aside,   100
    And with new joy and pride
The little actor cons another part,
Filling from time to time his 'humorous stage'
With all the persons down to palsied Age
That Life brings with her in her equipage –   105
    As if his whole vocation
    Were endless imitation.

Thou whose exterior semblance doth belie
    Thy soul's immensity;
Thou best philosopher who yet dost keep   110
Thy heritage; thou eye among the blind
That, deaf and silent, read'st the eternal deep,
Haunted forever by the eternal mind;
    Mighty prophet! Seer blessed!
      On whom those truths do rest   115
Which we are toiling all our lives to find;
Thou, over whom thy immortality
Broods like the day, a master o'er a slave,
A presence which is not to be put by,
      To whom the grave   120
Is but a lonely bed without the sense or sight
    Of day or the warm light,
A place of thought where we in waiting lie;
Thou little child, yet glorious in the might
Of untamed pleasures, on thy being's height –   125
Why with such earnest pains dost thou provoke
The years to bring the inevitable yoke,
Thus blindly with thy blessedness at strife?
Full soon thy soul shall have her earthly freight,

And custom lie upon thee with a weight   130
Heavy as frost, and deep almost as life.

    Oh joy! that in our embers
    Is something that doth live,
    That nature yet remembers
    What was so fugitive!   135
The thought of our past years in me doth breed
Perpetual benedictions, not indeed
For that which is most worthy to be blessed –
Delight and liberty, the simple creed
Of childhood, whether fluttering or at rest,   140
With new-born hope forever in his breast –
    Not for these I raise
    The song of thanks and praise;
   But for those obstinate questionings
    Of sense and outward things,   145
    Fallings from us, vanishings,
    Blank misgivings of a creature
Moving about in worlds not realized,
High instincts before which our mortal nature
Did tremble like a guilty thing surprised;   150
    But for those first affections,
    Those shadowy recollections
    Which, be they what they may,
Are yet the fountain-light of all our day,
Are yet a master-light of all our seeing;   155
    Uphold us, cherish us, and make
Our noisy years seem moments in the being
Of the eternal silence – truths that wake
    To perish never,
Which neither listlessness nor mad endeavour,   160
    Nor man nor boy,
Nor all that is at enmity with joy
Can utterly abolish or destroy!
  Hence, in a season of calm weather,
    Though inland far we be,   165
Our souls have sight of that immortal sea
    Which brought us hither,
    Can in a moment travel thither
And see the children sport upon the shore,
And hear the mighty waters rolling evermore.   170

Then sing, ye birds; sing, sing a joyous song!
    And let the young lambs bound
    As to the tabor's sound!
   We in thought will join your throng,
    Ye that pipe and ye that play,   175

Ye that through your hearts today
    Feel the gladness of the May!
What though the radiance which was once so bright
Be now for ever taken from my sight?
    Though nothing can bring back the hour   180
Of splendour in the grass, of glory in the flower,
        We will grieve not, rather find
        Strength in what remains behind,
        In the primal sympathy
        Which having been must ever be,   185
        In the soothing thoughts that spring
        Out of human suffering,
        In the faith that looks through death,
In years that bring the philosophic mind.

And oh, ye fountains, meadows, hills and groves,   190
Think not of any severing of our loves!
Yet in my heart of hearts I feel your might,
I only have relinquished one delight
To live beneath your more habitual sway.
I love the brooks which down their channels fret   195
Even more than when I tripped lightly as they;
The innocent brightness of a new-born day
            Is lovely yet;
The clouds that gather round the setting sun
Do take a sober colouring from an eye   200
That hath kept watch o'er man's mortality;
Another race hath been, and other palms are won.
Thanks to the human heart by which we live,
Thanks to its tenderness, its joys and fears,
To me the meanest flower that blows can give   205
Thoughts that do often lie too deep for tears.

Daffodils

I wandered lonely as a cloud
That floats on high o'er vales and hills,
When all at once I saw a crowd,
A host of dancing daffodils;
Along the lake, beneath the trees,   5
Ten thousand dancing in the breeze.

Continuous as the stars that shine
And twinkle on the milky way,
They stretched in never-ending line
Along the margin of a bay –   10

Ten thousand saw I at a glance,
Tossing their heads in sprightly dance.

The waves beside them danced, but they
Outdid the sparkling waves in glee;
A poet could not but be gay   15
In such a laughing company.
I gazed, and gazed, but little thought
What wealth the show to me had brought –

For oft when on my couch I lie
In vacant or in pensive mood,   20
They flash upon that inward eye
Which is the bliss of solitude,
And then my heart with pleasure fills,
And dances with the daffodils.

Stepping Westward

While my fellow-traveller and I were walking by the side of Loch Ketterine
one fine evening after sunset, in our road to a hut where, in the course of our
tour, we had been hospitably entertained some weeks before, we met in one
of the loneliest parts of that solitary region two well-dressed women, one of
whom said to us by way of greeting, 'What you are stepping westward?'

'What you are stepping westward?' 'Yea.'
'Twould be a wildish destiny
If we, who thus together roam
In a strange land, and far from home,
Were in this place the guests of Chance –   5
Yet who would stop, or fear to advance,
Though home or shelter he had none,
With such a sky to lead him on?

The dewy ground was dark and cold;
Behind, all gloomy to behold;   10
And stepping westward seemed to be
A kind of *heavenly* destiny.
I liked the greeting – 'twas a sound
Of something without place or bound,
And seemed to give me spiritual right   15
To travel through that region bright.

The voice was soft, and she who spake
Was walking by her native lake;
The salutation had to me
The very sound of courtesy: 20

Its power was felt, and while my eye
Was fixed upon the glowing sky,
The echo of the voice enwrought
A human sweetness with the thought
Of travelling through the world that lay   25
Before me in my endless way.

The Solitary Reaper

Behold her, single in the field,
Yon solitary highland lass!
Reaping and singing by herself –
Stop here, or gently pass!
Alone she cuts, and binds the grain,   5
And sings a melancholy strain;
Oh listen! for the vale profound
Is overflowing with the sound.

No nightingale did ever chaunt
So sweetly to reposing bands   10
Of travellers in some shady haunt
Among Arabian sands;
No sweeter voice was ever heard
In springtime from the cuckoo-bird,
Breaking the silence of the seas   15
Among the farthest Hebrides.

Will no one tell me what she sings?
Perhaps the plaintive numbers flow
For old, unhappy, far-off things
And battles long ago;   20
Or is it some more humble lay,
Familiar matter of today?
Some natural sorrow, loss, or pain
That has been, and may be again?

Whate'er the theme, the maiden sang   25
As if her song could have no ending;
I saw her singing at her work
And o'er the sickle bending;
I listened till I had my fill,
And as I mounted up the hill,   30
The music in my heart I bore
Long after it was heard no more.

The River Duddon: Conclusion

I thought of thee, my partner and my guide,
As being past away. Vain sympathies!
For *backward*, Duddon, as I cast my eyes,
I see what was, and is, and will abide;
Still glides the stream, and shall for ever glide;   5
The form remains, the function never dies,
While *we*, the brave, the mighty, and the wise,
We men who, in our morn of youth, defied
The elements, must vanish; be it so!
Enough, if something from our hands have power   10
To live, and act, and serve the future hour;
And if, as tow'rd the silent tomb we go,
Through love, through hope, and faith's transcendent dower,
We feel that we are greater than we know.

Samuel Taylor Coleridge
(1772–1834)

Of the Fragment of 'Kubla Khan'

The following fragment is here published at the request of a poet of great and deserved celebrity, and as far as the author's own opinions are concerned, rather as a psychological curiosity than on the ground of any supposed *poetic* merits.

In the summer of the year 1797, the author, then in ill health, had retired to a lonely farmhouse between Porlock and Lynton on the Exmoor confines of Somerset and Devonshire. In consequence of a slight indisposition, an anodyne had been prescribed, from the effects of which he fell asleep in his chair at the moment that he was reading the following sentence, or words of the same substance, in *Purchas's Pilgrimage*: 'Here the Khan Kubla commanded a palace to be built, and a stately garden thereunto. And thus ten miles of fertile ground were enclosed with a wall.'

The author continued for about three hours in a profound sleep (at least of the external senses) during which time he has the most vivid confidence that he could not have composed less than from two to three hundred lines – if that indeed can be called composition in which all the images rose up before him as *things*, with a parallel production of the correspondent expressions, without any sensation or consciousness of effort. On awaking he appeared to himself to have a distinct recollection of the whole, and taking his pen, ink, and paper, instantly and eagerly wrote down the lines that are here preserved. At this moment he was unfortunately called out by a person on business from Porlock and detained by him above an hour, and on his return to his room, found to his no small surprise and mortification that though he still retained some vague and dim recollection of the general purpose of the vision, yet, with the exception of some eight or ten scattered lines and images, all the rest had passed away like the images on the surface of a stream into which a stone has been cast – but, alas! without the after-restoration of the latter:

> Then all the charm
> Is broken – all that phantom-world so fair
> Vanishes, and a thousand circlets spread,
> And each misshapes the other. Stay awhile,
>   Poor youth, who scarcely dar'st lift up thine eyes –
> The stream will soon renew its smoothness, soon
> The visions will return! And lo, he stays,

> And soon the fragments dim of lovely forms
> Come trembling back, unite, and now once more
> The pool becomes a mirror.

Yet from the still-surviving recollections in his mind, the author has frequently purposed to finish for himself what had been originally, as it were, given to him. Σαμερον αδιον ασω,[1] but the tomorrow is yet to come.

As a contrast to this vision, I have annexed a fragment of a very different character, describing with equal fidelity the dream of pain and disease ['The Pains of Sleep'].

Kubla Khan

In Xanadu did Kubla Khan
A stately pleasure-dome decree,
Where Alph, the sacred river, ran
Through caverns measureless to man
   Down to a sunless sea.   5
So twice five miles of fertile ground
With walls and towers were girdled round;
And here were gardens bright with sinuous rills
Where blossomed many an incense-bearing tree;
And here were forests ancient as the hills,   10
And folding sunny spots of greenery.

But oh, that deep romantic chasm which slanted
Down the green hill athwart a cedarn cover!
A savage place, as holy and enchanted
As e'er beneath a waning moon was haunted   15
By woman wailing for her demon-lover!
And from this chasm, with ceaseless turmoil seething,
As if this earth in fast thick pants were breathing,
A mighty fountain momently was forced
Amid whose swift half-intermitted burst   20
Huge fragments vaulted like rebounding hail,
Or chaffy grain beneath the thresher's flail!
And mid these dancing rocks at once and ever,
It flung up momently the sacred river.
Five miles meandering with a mazy motion   25
Through wood and dale the sacred river ran,
Then reached the caverns measureless to man
And sank in tumult to a lifeless ocean.
And mid this tumult Kubla heard from far
Ancestral voices prophesying war!   30

---

[1] 'Today I shall sing more sweetly' (Theocritus, *Idyll* i 145).

The shadow of the dome of pleasure
Floated midway on the waves,
Where was heard the mingled measure
From the fountain and the caves;
It was a miracle of rare device,   35
A sunny pleasure-dome with caves of ice!

A damsel with a dulcimer
In a vision once I saw:
It was an Abyssinian maid
And on her dulcimer she played,   40
Singing of Mount Abora.
Could I revive within me
Her symphony and song,
To such a deep delight 'twould win me
That with music loud and long,   45
I would build that dome in air,
That sunny dome, those caves of ice!
And all who heard should see them there,
And all should cry, 'Beware, beware!
His flashing eyes, his floating hair!   50
Weave a circle round him thrice,
And close your eyes with holy dread
For he on honey-dew hath fed
And drank the milk of paradise.'

The Rime of the Ancient Mariner. In seven parts

Facile credo, plures esse Naturas invisibiles quam visibiles in rerum uni-
versitate. Sed horum omnium familiam quis nobis enarrabit? et gradus et
cognationes et discrimina et singulorum munera? Quid agunt? quae loca
habitant? Harum rerum notitiam semper ambivit ingenium humanum,
nunquam attigit. Juvat, interea, non diffiteor, quandoque in animo,
tanquam in Tabula, majoris et melioris mundi imaginem contemplari:
ne mens assuefacta hodiernae vitae minutiis se contrahat nimis, et tota
subsidat in pusillas cogitationes. Sed veritati interea invigilandum est,
modusque servandus, ut certa ab incertis, diem a nocte, distinguamus.[1]

             (Thomas Burnet, *Archaeologiae Philosophicae*
             [London, 1692], pp. 68–9)

---

[1] 'I can easily believe that there are more invisible than visible beings in the universe. But
who will describe to us their families, ranks, affinities, differences, and functions? What do
they do? Where do they live? The human mind has always sought knowledge of these
things, but has never attained it. I admit that it is good sometimes to contemplate in
thought, as in a picture, the image of a greater and better world; otherwise the mind, used
to the minor concerns of daily life, may contract itself too much, and concentrate entirely
on trivia. But meanwhile we must be vigilant for truth and moderation, that we may
distinguish certainty from doubt, day from night.'

Part the First

*An ancient mariner
  meeteth three
gallants bidden to a
  wedding-feast,
and detaineth one*

It is an ancient mariner,
And he stoppeth one of three:
'By thy long grey beard and glittering
        eye
Now wherefore stopp'st thou me?

The bridegroom's doors are opened
        wide,   5
And I am next of kin;
The guests are met, the feast is set –
Mayst hear the merry din.'

He holds him with his skinny hand,
'There was a ship', quoth he;   10
'Hold off! Unhand me, grey-beard
        loon!'
Eftsoons his hand dropped he.

*The wedding-guest is
  spellbound
by the eye of the old
  seafaring man,
and constrained to hear
  his tale.*

He holds him with his glittering eye –
The wedding-guest stood still,
And listens like a three years' child: 15
The mariner hath his will.

The wedding-guest sat on a stone,
He cannot choose but hear;
And thus spake on that ancient man,
The bright-eyed mariner: 20

'The ship was cheered, the harbour
        cleared,
Merrily did we drop
Below the kirk, below the hill,
Below the lighthouse top.

*The mariner tells how the ship
sailed southward with a good
  wind
and fair weather till it
  reached the
  line.*

The sun came up upon the left,   25
Out of the sea came he;
And he shone bright, and on the right
Went down into the sea.

Higher and higher every day,
Till over the mast at noon –'   30
The wedding-guest here beat his
        breast,
For he heard the loud bassoon.

<table>
<tr><td>

The wedding-guest heareth the bridal music, but the mariner continueth his tale.

</td><td>

The bride hath paced into the hall,
Red as a rose is she;
Nodding their heads before her goes   35
The merry minstrelsy.

The wedding-guest he beat his breast,
Yet he cannot choose but hear;
And thus spake on that ancient man,
The bright-eyed mariner.   40

</td></tr>
</table>

The ship drawn by a storm toward the south pole.

'And now the storm-blast came, and he
Was tyrannous and strong;
He struck with his o'ertaking wings,
And chased us south along.

With sloping masts and dipping prow,   45
As who pursued with yell and blow
Still treads the shadow of his foe
And forward bends his head,
The ship drove fast, loud roared the blast,
And southward aye we fled.   50

And now there came both mist and
    snow,
And it grew wondrous cold:
And ice mast-high came floating by
As green as emerald.

The land of ice, and of fearful sounds where no living thing was to be seen.

And through the drifts the snowy clift   55
Did send a dismal sheen;
Nor shapes of men nor beasts we ken –
The ice was all between.

The ice was here, the ice was there,
The ice was all around;   60
It cracked and growled, and roared and
    howled
Like noises in a swound.

At length did cross an albatross,
Thorough the fog it came;
As if it had been a Christian soul,
We hailed it in God's name.   65

Till a great sea-bird, called the albatross, came through the snow-fog, and was received with great hospitality.

It ate the food it ne'er had eat,
And round and round it flew:
The ice did split with a thunder-fit;
The helmsman steered us through.   70

*And lo! the albatross proveth
   a bird of
good omen, and followeth the
   ship as it returned northward
      through fog
   and floating ice.*

And a good south wind sprung up
      behind,
The albatross did follow;
And every day, for food or play,
Came to the mariners' hollo!

In mist or cloud, on mast or shroud,   75
It perched for vespers nine,
Whiles all the night, through
      fogsmoke white,
Glimmered the white moonshine.'

*The ancient mariner
   inhospitably killeth
the pious bird of good omen.*

'God save thee, ancient mariner,
From the fiends the plague thee thus!   80
Why look'st thou so?' 'With my
      crossbow
I shot the albatross.

Part the Second

The sun now rose upon the right,
Out of the sea came he;
Still hid in mist, and on the left   85
Went down into the sea.

And the good south wind still blew
      behind,
But no sweet bird did follow,
Nor any day for food or play
Came to the mariners' hollo!   90

*His shipmates cry out against
   the ancient
mariner, for killing the bird
of good luck.*

And I had done an hellish thing
And it would work 'em woe:
For all averred I had killed the bird
That made the breeze to blow.
"Ah wretch!" said they, "the bird to
      slay   95
That made the breeze to blow!"

*But when the fog cleared off,
   they justify
the same – and thus make
themselves accomplices in
   the crime.*

Nor dim nor red, like God's own
      head
The glorious sun uprist:
Then all averred I had killed the bird
That brought the fog and mist.   100
"'Twas right", said they, "such birds
      to slay,

That bring the fog and mist."

<table>
<tr><td>

*The fair breeze continues; the
ship enters
the Pacific Ocean and sails
northward, even till it reaches
the line.*

</td><td>

The fair breeze blew, the white foam
    flew,
The furrow [2] streamed off free:
We were the first that ever burst   105
Into that silent sea.

</td></tr>
</table>

*The ship hath been
suddenly becalmed.*

Down dropped the breeze, the sails
    dropped down,
'Twas sad as sad could be,
And we did speak only to break
The silence of the sea.   110

All in a hot and copper sky
The bloody sun at noon
Right up above the mast did stand,
No bigger than the moon.

Day after day, day after day,   115
We stuck, nor breath nor motion,
As idle as a painted ship
Upon a painted ocean.

*And the albatross begins
to be avenged.*

Water, water, everywhere,
And all the boards did shrink;   120
Water, water, everywhere,
Nor any drop to drink.

The very deeps did rot: oh Christ,
That ever this should be!
Yea, slimy things did crawl with legs   125
Upon the slimy sea.

About, about, in reel and rout
The death-fires danced at night;
The water, like a witch's oils,
Burnt green and blue and white.   130

---

[2] 'In the former edition the line was "The furrow followed free". But I had not been long on board a ship before I perceived that this was the image as seen by a spectator from the shore, or from another vessel. From the ship itself the wake appears like a brook flowing off from the stern' (C.).

A spirit had followed them; one of the invisible inhabitants of this planet, neither departed souls nor angels; concerning whom the learned Jew, Josephus, and the Platonic Constantinopolitan, Michael Psellus, may be consulted. They are very numerous, and there is no climate or element without one or more.

And some in dreams assured were
Of the spirit that plagued us so;
Nine fathom deep he had followed us
From the land of mist and snow.

And every tongue, through utter
 drought,   135
Was withered at the root;
We could not speak, no more than if
We had been choked with soot.

The shipmates in their sore distress would fain throw the whole guilt on the ancient mariner: in sign whereof they hang the dead sea-bird round his neck.

Ah wel-a-day! what evil looks
Had I from old and young! 140
Instead of the cross the albatross
About my neck was hung.

Part the Third

There passed a weary time. Each
 throat
Was parched, and glazed each eye.
A weary time! a weary time! 145
How glazed each weary eye!

The ancient mariner beholdeth a sign in the element afar off.

When looking westward, I beheld
A something in the sky.

At first it seemed a little speck
And then it seemed a mist; 150
It moved and moved, and took at
 last
A certain shape, I wist.

A speck, a mist, a shape, I wist!
And still it neared and neared:
And as if it dodged a water-sprite, 155
It plunged and tacked and veered.

At its nearer approach, it seemeth to him to be a ship; and at a dear ransom he freeth his speech from the bonds of thirst.

With throat unslaked, with black
 lips baked,
We could nor laugh nor wail;
Through utter drought all dumb
 we stood!
I bit my arm, I sucked the blood, 160
And cried, "A sail! A sail!"

With throat unslaked, with black lips
  baked,
Agape they heard me call:

A flash of joy.

Gramercy! they for joy did grin
And all at once their breath drew in   165
As they were drinking all.

And horror follows. For can it be a ship
that comes onward without wind or tide?

"See, see!" I cried, "She tacks no
  more,
Hither to work us weal;
Without a breeze, without a tide,
She steadies with upright keel."   170

The western wave was all a-flame,
The day was well nigh done!
Almost upon the western wave
Rested the broad bright sun;
When that strange shape drove
  suddenly   175
Betwixt us and the sun.

And straight the sun was flecked with
  bars

It seemeth him but the skeleton of a ship.

(Heaven's Mother send us grace!),
As if through a dungeon-grate he
  peered
With broad and burning face.   180

Alas! thought I, and my heart beat
  loud,
How fast she nears and nears!
Are those *her* sails that glance in the
  sun
Like restless gossameres?

And its ribs are seen as bars on the face of the setting sun.

Are those *her* ribs through which the
  sun   185
Did peer, as through a grate?

The spectre woman and her death-mate, and no other on board the skeleton-ship.

And is that woman all her crew?
Is that a Death? And are there two?
Is Death that woman's mate?

Like vessel, like crew!

Her lips were red, *her* looks were free,   190
Her locks were yellow as gold;
Her skin was as white as leprosy,
The nightmare Life-in-Death was she
Who thicks man's blood with cold.

<table>
<tr><td>

Death and Life-in-Death have diced
for the ship's crew, and she (the latter) winneth the ancient mariner.

</td><td>

The naked hulk alongside came,   195
And the twain were casting dice;
"The game is done! I've won! I've
        won!"
Quoth she, and whistles thrice.

</td></tr>
</table>

The sun's rim dips, the stars rush out,
At one stride comes the dark;   200
With far-heard whisper, o'er the sea,
Off shot the spectre-bark.

We listened and looked sideways up!
Fear at my heart, as at a cup,
My life-blood seemed to sip!   205
The stars were dim, and thick the
        night,
The steersman's face by his lamp
        gleamed white;

At the rising of the moon.

From the sails the dews did drip –
Till clomb above the eastern bar
The horned moon, with one bright
        star   210
Within the nether tip.

One after another,

One after one, by the star-dogged moon
Too quick for groan or sigh,
Each turned his face with a ghastly
        pang
And cursed me with his eye.   215

His shipmates drop down dead.

Four times fifty living men
(And I heard nor sigh nor groan)
With heavy thump, a lifeless lump,
They dropped down one by one.

But Life-in-Death begins her work
on the ancient mariner.

The souls did from their bodies fly,   220
They fled to bliss or woe!
And every soul, it passed me by
Like the whiz of my crossbow.'

Part the Fourth

The wedding-guest feareth
that a spirit is
talking to him;

'I fear thee, ancient mariner,
I fear thy skinny hand;   225
And thou art long and lank and brown
As is the ribbed sea-sand.

<table>
<tr><td>

But the ancient mariner assureth him of his bodily life, and proceedeth to relate his horrible penance.

</td><td>

I fear thee and thy glittering eye,
And thy skinny hand so brown – '
'Fear not, fear not, thou wedding-
    guest,   230
This body dropped not down.

</td></tr>
</table>

Alone, alone, all all alone,
Alone on a wide wide sea;
And never a saint took pity on
My soul in agony.   235

He despiseth the creatures of the calm,

The many men so beautiful,
And they all dead did lie!
And a thousand thousand slimy
    things
Lived on – and so did I.

And envieth that they should live, and so many lie dead.

I looked upon the rotting sea   240
And drew my eyes away;
I looked upon the rotting deck,
And there the dead men lay.

I looked to heaven and tried to pray
But or ever a prayer had gushed,   245
A wicked whisper came and made
My heart as dry as dust.

I closed my lids and kept them close
And the balls like pulses beat;
For the sky and the sea, and the sea
    and the sky   250
Lay like a load on my weary eye,
And the dead were at my feet.

But the curse liveth for him in the eye of the dead men

The cold sweat melted from their
    limbs,
Nor rot nor reek did they;
The look with which they looked on
    me   255
Had never passed away.

An orphan's curse would drag to hell
A spirit from on high;
But oh! more horrible than that
Is the curse in a dead man's eye!   260
Seven days, seven nights, I saw that
    curse
And yet I could not die.

In his loneliness and fixedness, he yearneth towards the journeying moon, and the stars that still sojourn, yet still move onward; and everywhere the blue sky belongs to them, and is their appointed rest, and their native country, and their own natural homes, which they enter unannounced, as lords that are certainly expected, and yet there is a silent joy at their arrival.

The moving moon went up the sky
And nowhere did abide;
Softly she was going up   265
And a star or two beside;

Her beams bemocked the sultry main
Like April hoar-frost spread;
But where the ship's huge shadow lay
The charmed water burnt alway   270
A still and awful red.

Beyond the shadow of the ship
I watched the water-snakes;
They moved in tracks of shining white,
And when they reared, the elfish light   275
Fell off in hoary flakes.

By the light of the moon he beholdeth God's creatures of the great calm.

Within the shadow of the ship
I watched their rich attire:
Blue, glossy green, and velvet black,
They coiled and swam, and every track   280
Was a flash of golden fire.

Their beauty and their happiness.

Oh happy living things! no tongue
Their beauty might declare:
A spring of love gushed from my heart

He blesseth them in his heart.

And I blessed them unaware!   285
Sure my kind saint took pity on me,
And I blessed them unaware.

The spell begins to break

The self-same moment I could pray,
And from my neck so free
The albatross fell off and sank   290
Like lead into the sea.

Part the Fifth

Oh sleep, it is a gentle thing
Beloved from pole to pole!
To Mary Queen the praise be given;
She sent the gentle sleep from heaven   295
That slid into my soul.

By grace of the holy Mother,
  the ancient
mariner is refreshed with
rain.

The silly buckets on the deck
That had so long remained,
I dreamt that they were filled with dew
And when I awoke it rained.   300

My lips were wet, my throat was cold,
My garments all were dank;
Sure I had drunken in my dreams
And still my body drank.

I moved and could not feel my limbs,   305
I was so light, almost
I thought that I had died in sleep
And was a blessed ghost.

He heareth sounds, and seeth
  strange
sights and commotions in
the sky and the element.

And soon I heard a roaring wind,   310
It did not come anear;
But with its sound it shook the sails
That were so thin and sere.

The upper air bursts into life
And a hundred fire-flags sheen,
To and fro they were hurried about;   315
And to and fro, and in and out
The wan stars danced between.

And the coming wind did roar more
      loud,
And the sails did sigh like sedge;
And the rain poured down from one
      black cloud,   320
The moon was at its edge.

The thick black cloud was cleft, and still
The moon was at its side;
Like waters shot from some high crag,
The lightning fell with never a jag,   325
A river steep and wide.

The bodies of the ship's crew are
inspirited, and the ship moves
  on;

The loud wind never reached the ship,
Yet now the ship moved on!
Beneath the lightning and the moon
The dead men gave a groan.   330

They groaned, they stirred, they all
      uprose,
Nor spake, nor moved their eyes;
It had been strange, even in a dream,
To have seen those dead men rise.

The helmsman steered, the ship moved
    on,   335
Yet never a breeze up-blew;
The mariners all 'gan work the ropes
Where they were wont to do;
They raised their limbs like lifeless tools –
We were a ghastly crew.   340

The body of my brother's son
Stood by me, knee to knee;
The body and I pulled at one rope
But he said nought to me.'

But not by the souls of the men,
    nor
by demons of earth or the
middle air, but by a blessed
    troop of
angelic spirits, sent down by the
invocation of the guardian saint.

'I fear thee, ancient mariner!'   345
'Be calm, thou wedding-guest!
'Twas not those souls that fled in pain,
Which to their corses came again,
But a troop of spirits blessed;

For when it dawned, they dropped their
    arms   350
And clustered round the mast;
Sweet sounds rose slowly through their
    mouths
And from their bodies passed.

Around, around, flew each sweet sound
Then darted to the sun;   355
Slowly the sounds came back again,
Now mixed, now one by one.

Sometimes a-dropping from the sky
I heard the skylark sing;
Sometimes all little birds that are,   360
How they seemed to fill the sea and air
With their sweet jargoning!

And now 'twas like all instruments,
Now like a lonely flute,
And now it is an angel's song   365
That makes the heavens be mute.

It ceased, yet still the sails made on
A pleasant noise till noon,
A noise like of a hidden brook
In the leafy month of June,   370
That to the sleeping woods all night
Singeth a quiet tune.

Till noon we quietly sailed on,
Yet never a breeze did breathe;
Slowly and smoothly went the ship,　　375
Moved onward from beneath.

The lonesome spirit from the
　South Pole
carries on the ship as far as the
line, in obedience to the angelic
　troop,
but still requireth vengeance.

Under the keel nine fathom deep,
From the land of mist and snow,
The spirit slid, and it was he
That made the ship to go.　　380
The sails at noon left off their tune
And the ship stood still also.

The sun right up above the mast
Had fixed her to the ocean;
But in a minute she 'gan stir　　385
With a short uneasy motion –
Backwards and forwards half her length,
With a short uneasy motion.

Then like a pawing horse let go,
She made a sudden bound;　　390
It flung the blood into my head,
And I fell down in a swound.

The Polar Spirit's fellow
　demons, the
invisible inhabitants of the
element, take part in his
　wrong; and two
of them relate, one to the
other, that penance long and
　heavy
for the ancient mariner hath
　been
accorded to the Polar Spirit,
　who
returneth southward.

How long in that same fit I lay,
I have not to declare;
But ere my living life returned,　　395
I heard and in my soul discerned
Two voices in the air.

"Is it he?" quoth one, "Is this the man?
By him who died on cross,
With his cruel bow he laid full low　　400
The harmless albatross.

The spirit who bideth by himself
In the land of mist and snow,
He loved the bird that loved the man
Who shot him with his bow."　　405

The other was a softer voice,
As soft as honey-dew;
Quoth he, "The man hath penance done
And penance more will do." '

Part the Sixth

FIRST VOICE

But tell me, tell me! speak again,   410
Thy soft response renewing –
What makes that ship drive on so fast?
What is the ocean doing?

SECOND VOICE

Still as a slave before his lord,
The ocean hath no blast;   415
His great bright eye most silently
Up to the moon is cast –

If he may know which way to go,
For she guides him smooth or grim.
See, brother, see – how graciously   420
She looketh down on him!

FIRST VOICE

The mariner hath been cast   But why drives on that ship so fast
into a trance;   Without or wave or wind?
for the angelic power
causeth the vessel to drive
northward,
faster than human life
could endure.

SECOND VOICE

The air is cut away before
And closes from behind.   425

Fly, brother, fly! more high, more
        high,
Or we shall be belated;
For slow and slow that ship will go
When the mariner's trance is abated.

The supernatural motion is   'I woke, and we were sailing on   430
retarded;   As in a gentle weather;
the mariner awakes, and   'Twas night, calm night, the moon
his penance begins anew.   was high –
                                 The dead men stood together.

All stood together on the deck,
For a charnel-dungeon fitter; 435
All fixed on me their stony eyes
That in the moon did glitter.

The pang, the curse, with which they
        died
Had never passed away;
I could not draw my eyes from theirs 440
Nor turn them up to pray.

The curse is finally expiated.   And now this spell was snapped;
                        once more
I viewed the ocean green,
And looked far forth, yet little saw
Of what had else been seen – 445

Like one that on a lonesome road
Doth walk in fear and dread,
And having once turned round walks on
And turns no more his head,
Because he knows a frightful fiend 450
Doth close behind him tread.

But soon there breathed a wind on me,
Nor sound nor motion made;
Its path was not upon the sea,
In ripple or in shade. 455

It raised my hair, it fanned my cheek,
Like a meadow-gale of spring –
It mingled strangely with my fears,
Yet it felt like a welcoming.

Swiftly, swiftly flew the ship, 460
Yet she sailed softly too;
Sweetly, sweetly blew the breeze –
On me alone it blew.

And the ancient mariner   Oh dream of joy! Is this indeed
beholdeth his   The lighthouse top I see? 465
native country.   Is this the hill? Is this the kirk?
Is this mine own countree?

We drifted o'er the harbour-bar,
And I with sobs did pray,
"Oh let me be awake, my God! 470
Or let me sleep alway!"

The harbour-bay was clear as glass,
So smoothly it was strewn!
And on the bay the moonlight lay
And the shadow of the moon.   475

The rock shone bright, the kirk no less
That stands above the rock;
The moonlight steeped in silentness
The steady weathercock.

And the bay was white with silent
        light,   480
Till rising from the same,

*The angelic spirits leave the
dead bodies,*
Full many shapes that shadows were
In crimson colours came.

*And appear in their own
forms of light.*
A little distance from the prow
Those crimson shadows were;   485
I turned my eyes upon the deck –
Oh Christ! What saw I there!

Each corse lay flat, lifeless and flat,
And by the holy rood,
A man all light, a seraph-man   490
On every corse there stood.

This seraph-band, each waved his hand –
It was a heavenly sight!
They stood as signals to the land,
Each one a lovely light;   495

This seraph-band, each waved his hand,
No voice did they impart –
No voice, but oh! the silence sank
Like music on my heart.

But soon I heard the dash of oars,   500
I heard the pilot's cheer;
My head was turned perforce away
And I saw a boat appear.

The pilot and the pilot's boy,
I heard them coming fast –   505
Dear Lord in heaven! it was a joy
The dead men could not blast.

I saw a third, I heard his voice –
It is the hermit good!

He singeth loud his godly hymns 510
That he makes in the wood.
He'll shrieve my soul, he'll wash away
The albatross's blood.

Part the Seventh

The hermit of the wood,

This hermit good lives in that wood
Which slopes down to the sea; 515
How loudly his sweet voice he rears!
He loves to talk with mariners
That come from a far countree.

He kneels at morn, and noon and eve,
He hath a cushion plump; 520
It is the moss that wholly hides
The rotted old oak-stump.

The skiff-boat neared, I heard them talk.
"Why, this is strange, I trow!
Where are those lights so many and
fair, 525
That signal made but now?"

Approacheth the ship with
wonder.

"Strange, by my faith!" the hermit said,
"And they answered not our cheer!
The planks look warped, and see those
sails,
How thin they are and sere! 530
I never saw aught like to them
Unless perchance it were

The skeletons of leaves that lag
My forest brook along,
When the ivy-tod is heavy with snow 535
And the owlet whoops to the wolf below
That eats the she-wolf's young."

"Dear Lord! it hath a fiendish look",
The pilot made reply,
"I am a-feared." "Push on, push on!" 540
Said the hermit cheerily.

The boat came closer to the ship
But I nor spake nor stirred;
The boat came close beneath the ship
And straight a sound was heard! 545

The ship suddenly sinketh.

Under the water it rumbled on,
Still louder and more dread;
It reached the ship, it split the bay –
The ship went down like lead.

*The ancient mariner is
saved in the
pilot's boat.*

Stunned by that loud and dreadful
    sound   550
Which sky and ocean smote,
Like one that hath been seven days
    drowned,
My body lay afloat;
But swift as dreams, myself I found
Within the pilot's boat.   555

Upon the whirl where sank the ship
The boat spun round and round,
And all was still, save that the hill
Was telling of the sound.

I moved my lips – the pilot shrieked   560
And fell down in a fit;
The holy hermit raised his eyes
And prayed where he did sit.

I took the oars; the pilot's boy,
Who now doth crazy go,   565
Laughed loud and long, and all the
    while
His eyes went to and fro:
"Ha! ha!" quoth he, "full plain I see
The Devil knows how to row."

And now all in my own countrée   570
I stood on the firm land!
The hermit stepped forth from the boat,
And scarcely he could stand.

*The ancient mariner earnestly
  entreateth
the hermit to shrieve
him; and the penance of life
  falls on
him.*

"Oh shrieve me, shrieve me, holy
    man!"
The hermit crossed his brow.   575
"Say quick", quoth he, "I bid thee
    say
What manner of man art thou?"
Forthwith this frame of mine was
    wrenched
With a woeful agony,
Which forced me to begin my tale –   580
And then it left me free.

And ever and anon throughout his future life an agony constraineth him to travel from land to land,

Since then, at an uncertain hour,
That agony returns,
And till my ghastly tale is told,
This heart within me burns.   585

I pass, like night, from land to land,
I have strange power of speech;
The moment that his face I see,
I know the man that must hear me –
To him my tale I teach.   590

What loud uproar bursts from that door!
The wedding-guests are there;
But in the garden bower the bride
And bridemaids singing are;
And hark, the little vesper-bell   595
Which biddeth me to prayer.
Oh wedding-guest! this soul hath been
Alone on a wide wide sea;
So lonely 'twas, that God himself
Scarce seemed there to be.   600

Oh sweeter than the marriage-feast,
'Tis sweeter far to me
To walk together to the kirk
With a goodly company!

To walk together to the kirk   605
And all together pray,
While each to his great Father bends,
Old men, and babes, and loving friends,
And youths and maidens gay.

And to teach by his own example love and reverence to all things that God made and loveth.

Farewell, farewell! but this I tell   610
To thee, thou wedding-guest!
He prayeth well who loveth well
Both man and bird and beast.

He prayeth best who loveth best
All things both great and small,   615
For the dear God who loveth us,
He made and loveth all.'

The mariner, whose eye is bright,
Whose beard with age is hoar,
Is gone; and now the wedding-guest   620
Turned from the bridegroom's door.

He went like one that hath been stunned
And is of sense forlorn:
A sadder and a wiser man
He rose the morrow morn.   625

Frost at Midnight

The frost performs its secret ministry
Unhelped by any wind. The owlet's cry
Came loud – and hark, again! loud as before.
The inmates of my cottage, all at rest,
Have left me to that solitude which suits   5
Abstruser musings, save that at my side
My cradled infant slumbers peacefully.
'Tis calm indeed! – so calm that it disturbs
And vexes meditation with its strange
And extreme silentness. Sea, hill, and wood,   10
This populous village! Sea, and hill, and wood,
With all the numberless goings-on of life,
Inaudible as dreams! The thin blue flame
Lies on my low-burnt fire, and quivers not;
Only that film[1] which fluttered on the grate   15
Still flutters there, the sole unquiet thing.
Methinks its motion in this hush of nature
Gives it dim sympathies with me who live,
Making it a companionable form
Whose puny flaps and freaks the idling spirit   20
By its own moods interprets, everywhere
Echo or mirror seeking of itself,
And makes a toy of thought.
                          But oh, how oft,
How oft at school, with most believing mind,
Presageful, have I gazed upon the bars,   25
To watch that fluttering stranger! And as oft
With unclosed lids, already had I dreamt
Of my sweet birthplace, and the old church-tower
Whose bells, the poor man's only music, rang
From morn to evening all the hot fair-day,   30
So sweetly that they stirred and haunted me
With a wild pleasure, falling on mine ear
Most like articulate sounds of things to come!
So gazed I till the soothing things I dreamt
Lulled me to sleep, and sleep prolonged my dreams!   35
And so I brooded all the following morn,

---

[1] 'In all parts of the kingdom these films are called "strangers", and supposed to portend
the arrival of some absent friend' (C.).

Awed by the stern preceptor's face, mine eye
Fixed with mock study on my swimming book;
Save if the door half opened, and I snatched
A hasty glance, and still my heart leaped up,   40
For still I hoped to see the stranger's face –
Townsman, or aunt, or sister more beloved,
My playmate when we both were clothed alike!

    Dear babe, that sleepest cradled by my side,
Whose gentle breathings heard in this deep calm   45
Fill up the interspersed vacancies
And momentary pauses of the thought;
My babe so beautiful, it fills my heart
With tender gladness thus to look at thee,
And think that thou shalt learn far other lore   50
And in far other scenes! For I was reared
In the great city, pent mid cloisters dim,
And saw nought lovely but the sky and stars.
But thou, my babe, shalt wander like a breeze
By lakes and sandy shores, beneath the crags   55
Of ancient mountain, and beneath the clouds
Which image in their bulk both lakes and shores
And mountain crags; so shalt thou see and hear
The lovely shapes and sounds intelligible
Of that eternal language which thy God   60
Utters, who from eternity doth teach
Himself in all, and all things in himself.
Great universal teacher! He shall mould
Thy spirit, and by giving make it ask.

    Therefore all seasons shall be sweet to thee,   65
Whether the summer clothe the general earth
With greenness, or the redbreast sit and sing
Betwixt the tufts of snow on the bare branch
Of mossy apple-tree, while the nigh thatch
Smokes in the sun-thaw; whether the eave-drops fall   70
Heard only in the trances of the blast,
Or if the secret ministry of frost
Shall hang them up in silent icicles,
Quietly shining to the quiet moon.

Christabel (Part I and conclusion only)

Part I

'Tis the middle of night by the castle clock,
And the owls have awakened the crowing cock;
Tu-whit! Tu-whoo!

And hark, again! the crowing cock,
How drowsily it crew.   5

Sir Leoline, the Baron rich,
Hath a toothless mastiff bitch;
From her kennel beneath the rock
She makes answer to the clock –
Four for the quarters and twelve for the hour,   10
Ever and aye, moonshine or shower,
Sixteen short howls not over loud;
Some say she sees my lady's shroud.

Is the night chilly and dark?
The night is chilly, but not dark –   15
The thin grey cloud is spread on high,
It covers but not hides the sky.
The moon is behind, and at the full,
And yet she looks both small and dull;
The night is chill, the cloud is grey –   20
'Tis a month before the month of May
And the spring comes slowly up this way.

The lovely lady, Christabel,
Whom her father loves so well,
What makes her in the wood so late,   25
A furlong from the castle gate?
She had dreams all yesternight
Of her own betrothed knight –
Dreams that made her moan and leap
As on her bed she lay in sleep;   30
And she in the midnight wood will pray
For the weal of her lover that's far away.

She stole along, she nothing spoke,
The breezes they were still also;
And nought was green upon the oak   35
But moss and rarest mistletoe;
She kneels beneath the huge oak tree
And in silence prayeth she.
The lady leaps up suddenly,
The lovely lady, Christabel!   40
It moaned as near as near can be,
But what it is, she cannot tell:
On the other side it seems to be
Of the huge, broad-breasted, old oak tree.

The night is chill, the forest bare –   45
Is it the wind that moaneth bleak?

There is not wind enough in the air
To move away the ringlet curl
From the lovely lady's cheek;
There is not wind enough to twirl   50
The one red leaf, the last of its clan,
That dances as often as dance it can,
Hanging so light and hanging so high
On the topmost twig that looks up at the sky.

Hush, beating heart of Christabel!   55
Jesu Maria, shield her well!
She folded her arms beneath her cloak
And stole to the other side of the oak:
    What sees she there?
There she sees a damsel bright   60
Dressed in a silken robe of white;
Her neck, her feet, her arms were bare,
And the jewels disordered in her hair.
I guess 'twas frightful there to see
A lady so richly clad as she –   65
Beautiful exceedingly!

'Mary mother, save me now!'
Said Christabel, 'And who art thou?'

The lady strange made answer meet
And her voice was faint and sweet.   70
'Have pity on my sore distress,
I scarce can speak for weariness!'
'Stretch forth thy hand, and have no fear',
Said Christabel, 'How cam'st thou here?'
And the lady whose voice was faint and sweet   75
Did thus pursue her answer meet:

'My sire is of a noble line,
And my name is Geraldine.
Five warriors seized me yestermorn –
Me, even me, a maid forlorn;   80
They choked my cries with force and fright
And tied me on a palfrey white.
The palfrey was as fleet as wind,
And they rode furiously behind.
They spurred amain, their steeds were white,   85
And once we crossed the shade of night.
As sure as Heaven shall rescue me,
I have no thought what men they be;
Nor do I know how long it is
(For I have lain in fits, I wis)   90

Since one, the tallest of the five,
Took me from the palfrey's back,
A weary woman scarce alive.
Some muttered words his comrades spoke,
He placed me underneath this oak,   95
He swore they would return with haste;
Whither they went I cannot tell –
I thought I heard, some minutes past,
Sounds as of a castle-bell.
Stretch forth thy hand (thus ended she)   100
And help a wretched maid to flee.'
Then Christabel stretched forth her hand
And comforted fair Geraldine,
Saying that she should command
The service of Sir Leoline,   105
And straight be convoyed, free from thrall,
Back to her noble father's hall.

So up she rose and forth they passed
With hurrying steps, yet nothing fast;
Her lucky stars the lady blessed,   110
And Christabel, she sweetly said,
'All our household are at rest,
Each one sleeping in his bed.
Sir Leoline is weak in health
And may not well awakened be,   115
So to my room we'll creep in stealth
And you tonight must sleep with me.'

They crossed the moat, and Christabel
Took the key that fitted well –
A little door she opened straight   120
All in the middle of the gate,
The gate that was ironed within and without
Where an army in battle array had marched out.

The lady sank, belike through pain,
And Christabel with might and main   125
Lifted her up, a weary weight,
Over the threshold of the gate;
Then the lady rose again
And moved as she were not in pain.

So free from danger, free from fear,   130
They crossed the court – right glad they were.
And Christabel devoutly cried
To the lady by her side,
'Praise we the Virgin all divine

Who hath rescued thee from thy distress!'   135
'Alas, alas,' said Geraldine,
'I cannot speak for weariness.'
So free from danger, free from fear,
They crossed the court – right glad they were.

Outside her kennel, the mastiff old   140
Lay fast asleep in moonshine cold.
The mastiff old did not awake,
Yet she an angry moan did make.
And what can ail the mastiff bitch?
Never till now she uttered yell   145
Beneath the eye of Christabel.
Perhaps it is the owlet's scritch,
For what can ail the mastiff bitch?

They passed the hall that echoes still,
Pass as lightly as you will.   150
The brands were flat, the brands were dying,
Amid their own white ashes lying;
But when the lady passed, there came
A tongue of light, a fit of flame,
And Christabel saw the lady's eye,   155
And nothing else saw she thereby
Save the boss of the shield of Sir Leoline tall
Which hung in a murky old nitch in the wall.
'Oh softly tread', said Christabel,
'My father seldom sleepeth well.'   160

Sweet Christabel, her feet she bares
And they are creeping up the stairs,
Now in glimmer and now in gloom,
And now they pass the Baron's room,
As still as death with stifled breath;   165
And now have reached her chamber door,
And now with eager feet press down
The rushes of her chamber floor.

The moon shines dim in the open air
And not a moonbeam enters here.   170
But they without its light can see
The chamber carved so curiously,
Carved with figures strange and sweet
All made out of the carver's brain
For a lady's chamber meet;   175
The lamp with twofold silver chain
Is fastened to an angel's feet.

The silver lamp burns dead and dim,
But Christabel the lamp will trim.
She trimmed the lamp and made it bright   180
And left it swinging to and fro,
While Geraldine in wretched plight
Sank down upon the floor below.
'Oh weary lady Geraldine,
I pray you, drink this cordial wine.   185
It is a wine of virtuous powers –
My mother made it of wild-flowers.'

'And will your mother pity me,
Who am a maiden most forlorn?'
Christabel answered, 'Woe is me!   190
She died the hour that I was born.
I have heard the grey-haired friar tell
How on her deathbed she did say
That she should hear the castle bell
Strike twelve upon my wedding day.   195
Oh mother dear, that thou wert here!'
'I would', said Geraldine, 'she were.'

But soon with altered voice said she,
'Off, wandering mother! Peak and pine!
I have power to bid thee flee.'   200
Alas, what ails poor Geraldine?
Why stares she with unsettled eye?
Can she the bodiless dead espy?
And why with hollow voice cries she,
'Off, woman, off! this hour is mine –   205
Though thou her guardian spirit be,
Off, woman, off! – 'tis given to me'?

Then Christabel knelt by the lady's side,
And raised to heaven her eyes so blue;
'Alas!' said she, 'this ghastly ride –   210
Dear lady, it hath wildered you!'
The lady wiped her moist cold brow,
And faintly said, ''Tis over now!'

Again the wild-flower wine she drank;
Her fair large eyes 'gan glitter bright,   215
And from the floor whereon she sank,
The lofty lady stood upright:
She was most beautiful to see,
Like a lady of a far countrée.

And thus the lofty lady spake: 220
'All they who live in the upper sky

Do love you, holy Christabel!
And you love them, and for their sake,
And for the good which me befell,
Even I, in my degree will try,   225
Fair maiden, to requite you well.
But now unrobe yourself, for I
Must pray, ere yet in bed I lie.'

Quoth Christabel, 'So let it be!'
And as the lady bade, did she.   230
Her gentle limbs did she undress,
And lay down in her loveliness.

But through her brain, of weal and woe
So many thoughts moved to and fro
That vain it were her lids to close;   235
So halfway from the bed she rose,
And on her elbow did recline
To look at the lady Geraldine.

Beneath the lamp the lady bowed
And slowly rolled her eyes around;   240
Then drawing in her breath aloud
Like one that shuddered, she unbound
The cincture from beneath her breast:
Her silken robe and inner vest
Dropped to her feet, and full in view,   245
Behold! her bosom and half her side –
A sight to dream of, not to tell!
And she is to sleep by Christabel.

She took two paces and a stride,
And lay down by the maiden's side;   250
And in her arms the maid she took,
        Ah wel-a-day!
And with low voice and doleful look
        These words did say:
'In the touch of this bosom there worketh a spell   255
Which is lord of thy utterance, Christabel!
Thou knowest tonight, and wilt know tomorrow,
This mark of my shame, this seal of my sorrow;
    But vainly thou warrest,
        For this is alone in   260
    Thy power to declare,
        That in the dim forest
        Thou heard'st a low moaning,
And found'st a bright lady surpassingly fair,

And didst bring her home with thee in love and in
    charity,   265
To shield her and shelter her from the damp air.'

The Conclusion to Part I

It was a lovely sight to see
The lady Christabel, when she
Was praying at the old oak tree.
    Amid the jagged shadows   270
    Of mossy leafless boughs,
    Kneeling in the moonlight
    To make her gentle vows;
Her slender palms together pressed,
Heaving sometimes on her breast;   275
Her face resigned to bliss or bale,
Her face – oh call it fair, not pale!
And both blue eyes more bright than clear,
Each about to have a tear.

With open eyes (ah woe is me!)   280
Asleep, and dreaming fearfully,
Fearfully dreaming, yet I wis,
Dreaming that alone, which is –
Oh sorrow and shame! Can this be she,
The lady who knelt at the old oak tree?   285
And lo! the worker of these harms
That holds the maiden in her arms,
Seems to slumber still and mild,
As a mother with her child.

A star hath set, a star hath risen,   290
Oh Geraldine, since arms of thine
Have been the lovely lady's prison!
Oh Geraldine, one hour was thine –
Thou'st had thy will! By tairn and rill
The night-birds all that hour were still;   295
But now they are jubilant anew,
From cliff and tower, tu-whoo! tu-whoo!
Tu-whoo! tu-whoo! from wood and fell!

And see! the lady Christabel
Gathers herself from out her trance;   300
Her limbs relax, her countenance
Grows sad and soft; the smooth thin lids
Close o'er her eyes, and tears she sheds –

Large tears that leave the lashes bright;
And oft the while she seems to smile   305
As infants at a sudden light!

Yea she doth smile and she doth weep
Like a youthful hermitess
Beauteous in a wilderness,
Who praying always, prays in sleep.   310
And if she move unquietly,
Perchance 'tis but the blood so free
Comes back and tingles in her feet.
No doubt she hath a vision sweet:
What if her guardian spirit 'twere?   315
What if she knew her mother near?
But this she knows – in joys and woes,
That saints will aid if men will call,
For the blue sky bends over all.

George Gordon Byron, 6th Baron Byron (1788–1824)

Don Juan

Canto II

1

Oh ye who teach the ingenuous youth of nations –
   Holland, France, England, Germany, or Spain –
I pray ye flog them upon all occasions:
   It mends their morals, never mind the pain!
The best of mothers and of educations   5
   In Juan's case were but employed in vain,
Since, in a way that's rather of the oddest, he
Became divested of his native modesty.

2

Had he but been placed at a public school,
   In the third form, or even in the fourth,   10
His daily task had kept his fancy cool,
   At least, had he been nurtured in the north;
Spain may prove an exception to the rule,
   But then exceptions always prove its worth –
A lad of sixteen causing a divorce   15
Puzzled his tutors very much, of course.

3

I can't say that it puzzles me at all,
   If all things be considered: first there was
His lady-mother, mathematical,
   A – never mind; his tutor, an old ass;   20
A pretty woman (that's quite natural,
   Or else the thing had hardly come to pass);
A husband rather old, not much in unity
With his young wife; a time, and opportunity.

4

Well – well, the world must turn upon its axis,   25
    And all mankind turn with it, heads or tails,
And live and die, make love and pay our taxes,
    And, as the veering wind shifts, shift our sails;
The king commands us, and the doctor quacks us,
    The priest instructs, and so our life exhales   30
A little breath, love, wine, ambition, fame,
Fighting, devotion, dust, perhaps a name.

5

I said that Juan had been sent to Cadiz –
    A pretty town, I recollect it well –
'Tis there the mart of the colonial trade is   35
    (Or was, before Peru learned to rebel);
And such sweet girls – I mean, such graceful ladies,
    Their very walk would make your bosom swell;
I can't describe it, though so much it strike,
Nor liken it – I never saw the like: 40

6

An Arab horse, a stately stag, a barb
    New broke, a cameleopard, a gazelle –
No, none of these will do – and then their garb,
    Their veil and petticoat! (Alas, to dwell
Upon such things would very near absorb   45
    A canto!) Then their feet and ankles – well,
Thank heaven I've got no metaphor quite ready
(And so, my sober muse, come, let's be steady,

7

Chaste Muse! – Well, if you must, you must); the veil
    Thrown back a moment with the glancing hand,   50
While the o'erpowering eye that turns you pale
    Flashes into the heart. All sunny land
Of love, when I forget you, may I fail
    To – say my prayers; but never was there planned
A dress through which the eyes give such a volley,   55
Excepting the Venetian fazzioli.

8

But to our tale: the Donna Inez sent
    Her son to Cadiz only to embark;
To stay there had not answered her intent,
    But why? We leave the reader in the dark –   60
'Twas for a voyage that the young man was meant,
    As if a Spanish ship were Noah's ark,

To wean him from the wickedness of earth
And send him like a dove of promise forth.

9

Don Juan bade his valet pack his things   65
   According to direction, then received
A lecture and some money: for four springs
   He was to travel, and though Inez grieved
(As every kind of parting has its stings),
   She hoped he would improve – perhaps believed: 70
A letter, too, she gave (he never read it)
Of good advice – and two or three of credit.

10

In the meantime, to pass her hours away,
   Brave Inez now set up a Sunday school
For naughty children, who would rather play   75
   (Like truant rogues) the devil or the fool;
Infants of three years old were taught that day,
   Dunces were whipped, or set upon a stool:
The great success of Juan's education
Spurred her to teach another generation.   80

11

Juan embarked, the ship got under way,
   The wind was fair, the water passing rough;
A devil of a sea rolls in that bay,
   As I, who've crossed it oft, know well enough;
And, standing upon deck, the dashing spray   85
   Flies in one's face, and makes it weather-tough:
And there he stood to take, and take again,
His first, perhaps his last, farewell of Spain.

12

I can't but say it is an awkward sight
   To see one's native land receding through   90
The growing waters; it unmans one quite,
   Especially when life is rather new.
I recollect Great Britain's coast looks white,
   But almost every other country's blue,
When gazing on them, mystified by distance,   95
We enter on our nautical existence.

13

So Juan stood, bewildered, on the deck:
   The wind sung, cordage strained, and sailors swore,
And the ship creaked, the town became a speck,
   From which away so fair and fast they bore.   100

The best of remedies is a beefsteak
    Against seasickness; try it, sir, before
You sneer, and I assure you this is true,
For I have found it answer – so may you.

14

Don Juan stood and, gazing from the stern,   105
    Beheld his native Spain receding far.
First partings form a lesson hard to learn,
    Even nations feel this when they go to war;
There is a sort of unexpressed concern,
    A kind of shock that sets one's heart ajar: 110
At leaving even the most unpleasant people
And places, one keeps looking at the steeple.

15

But Juan had got many things to leave,
    His mother, and a mistress, and no wife,
So that he had much better cause to grieve   115
    Than many persons more advanced in life;
And if we now and then a sigh must heave
    At quitting even those we quit in strife,
No doubt we weep for those the heart endears –
That is, till deeper griefs congeal our tears.   120

16

So Juan wept, as wept the captive Jews
    By Babel's waters, still remembering Zion:
I'd weep, but mine is not a weeping muse,
    And such light griefs are not a thing to die on;
Young men should travel, if but to amuse   125
    Themselves – and the next time their servants tie on
Behind their carriages their new portmanteau,
Perhaps it may be lined with this my canto

17

And Juan wept, and much he sighed and thought,
    While his salt tears dropped into the salt sea,   130
'Sweets to the sweet' (I like so much to quote;
    You must excuse this extract – 'tis where she,
The Queen of Denmark, for Ophelia brought
    Flowers to the grave), and, sobbing often, he
Reflected on his present situation,   135
And seriously resolved on reformation.

18

'Farewell, my Spain, a long farewell!' he cried,
    'Perhaps I may revisit thee no more,

But die, as many an exiled heart hath died,
    Of its own thirst to see again thy shore;   140
Farewell, where Guadalquivir's waters glide!
    Farewell, my mother! And, since all is o'er,
Farewell, too dearest Julia!' (Here he drew
Her letter out again, and read it through.)

19

'And oh, if e'er I should forget, I swear –   145
    But that's impossible, and cannot be –
Sooner shall this blue ocean melt to air,
    Sooner shall earth resolve itself to sea,
Than I resign thine image, oh my fair!
    Or think of anything excepting thee;   150
A mind diseased no remedy can physic – '
(Here the ship gave a lurch, and he grew seasick.)

20

'Sooner shall heaven kiss earth – ' (Here he fell sicker)
    'Oh Julia, what is every other woe?
(For God's sake let me have a glass of liquor,   155
    Pedro, Battista, help me down below!)
Julia, my love! – you rascal, Pedro, quicker –
    Oh Julia! – this cursed vessel pitches so –
Beloved Julia, hear me still beseeching!'
(Here he grew inarticulate with reaching.)   160

21

He felt that chilling heaviness of heart,
    Or rather stomach – which, alas, attends,
Beyond the best apothecary's art,
    The loss of love, the treachery of friends,
Or death of those we dote on, when a part   165
    Of us dies with them as each fond hope ends:
No doubt he would have been much more pathetic,
But the sea acted as a strong emetic.

22

Love's a capricious power; I've known it hold
    Out through a fever caused by its own heat,   170
But be much puzzled by a cough and cold,
    And find a quinsy very hard to treat;
Against all noble maladies he's bold,
    But vulgar illnesses don't like to meet –
Nor that a sneeze should interrupt his sigh,   175
Nor inflammations redden his blind eye.

23

But worst of all is nausea, or a pain
   About the lower region of the bowels;
Love, who heroically breathes a vein,
   Shrinks from the application of hot towels,   180
And purgatives are dangerous to his reign,
   Seasickness death: his love was perfect, how else
Could Juan's passion, while the billows roar,
Resist his stomach, ne'er at sea before?

24

The ship, called the most holy *Trinidada*,   185
   Was steering duly for the port Leghorn,
For there the Spanish family Moncada
   Were settled long ere Juan's sire was born:
They were relations, and for them he had a
   Letter of introduction, which the morn   190
Of his departure had been sent him by
His Spanish friends for those in Italy.

25

His suite consisted of three servants and
   A tutor – the licentiate Pedrillo,
Who several languages did understand,   195
   But now lay sick and speechless on his pillow,
And, rocking in his hammock, longed for land,
   His headache being increased by every billow;
And the waves oozing through the porthole made
His berth a little damp, and him afraid.   200

26

'Twas not without some reason, for the wind
   Increased at night until it blew a gale;
And though 'twas not much to a naval mind,
   Some landsmen would have looked a little pale –
For sailors are, in fact, a different kind.   205
   At sunset they began to take in sail,
For the sky showed it would come on to blow,
And carry away, perhaps, a mast or so.

27

At one o'clock the wind with sudden shift
   Threw the ship right into the trough of the sea,   210
Which struck her aft, and made an awkward rift,
   Started the stern-post, also shattered the
Whole of her stern-frame, and ere she could lift
   Herself from out her present jeopardy

The rudder tore away: 'twas time to sound   215
The pumps, and there were four feet water found.

28

One gang of people instantly was put
    Upon the pumps, and the remainder set
To get up part of the cargo, and what-not,
    But they could not come at the leak as yet;   220
At last they did get at it really, but
    Still their salvation was an even bet.
The water rushed through in a way quite puzzling,
While they thrust sheets, shirts, jackets, bales of muslin

29

Into the opening – but all such ingredients   225
    Would have been vain, and they must have gone down,
Despite of all their efforts and expedients,
    But for the pumps: I'm glad to make them known
To all the brother tars who may have need hence,
    For fifty tons of water were upthrown   230
By them per hour, and they had all been undone
But for their maker, Mr Mann, of London.

30

As day advanced the weather seemed to abate,
    And then the leak they reckoned to reduce,
And keep the ship afloat, though three feet yet   235
    Kept two hand-and one chain-pump still in use.
The wind blew fresh again: as it grew late
    A squall came on, and while some guns broke loose,
A gust, which all descriptive power transcends,
Laid with one blast the ship on her beam-ends.   240

31

There she lay, motionless, and seemed upset;
    The water left the hold, and washed the decks,
And made a scene men do not soon forget;
    For they remember battles, fires, and wrecks,
Or any other thing that brings regret,   245
    Or breaks their hopes, or hearts, or heads, or necks:
Thus drownings are much talked of by the divers
And swimmers who may chance to be survivors.

32

Immediately the masts were cut away,
    Both main and mizen; first the mizen went,   250
The mainmast followed. But the ship still lay
    Like a mere log, and baffled our intent.

Foremast and bowsprit were cut down, and they
    Eased her at last (although we never meant
To part with all till every hope was blighted),   255
And then with violence the old ship righted.

33

It may be easily supposed, while this
    Was going on, some people were unquiet,
That passengers would find it much amiss
    To lose their lives as well as spoil their diet;   260
That even the able seaman, deeming his
    Days nearly o'er, might be disposed to riot,
As upon such occasions tars will ask
For grog, and sometimes drink rum from the cask.

34

There's nought, no doubt, so much the spirit calms   265
    As rum and true religion; thus it was
Some plundered, some drank spirits, some sung psalms,
    The high wind made the treble, and as bass
The hoarse harsh waves kept time; fright cured the qualms
    Of all the luckless landsmen's seasick maws: 270
Strange sounds of wailing, blasphemy, devotion,
Clamoured in chorus to the roaring ocean.

35

Perhaps more mischief had been done, but for
    Our Juan who, with sense beyond his years,
Got to the spirit-room, and stood before   275
    It with a pair of pistols; and their fears,
As if Death were more dreadful by his door
    Of fire than water, spite of oaths and tears,
Kept still aloof the crew who, ere they sunk,
Thought it would be becoming to die drunk.   280

36

'Give us more grog', they cried, 'for it will be
    All one an hour hence.' Juan answered, 'No!
'Tis true that death awaits both you and me,
    But let us die like men, not sink below
Like brutes.' And thus his dangerous post kept he,   285
    And none liked to anticipate the blow;
And even Pedrillo, his most reverend tutor,
Was for some rum a disappointed suitor.

37

The good old gentleman was quite aghast
    And made a loud and a pious lamentation,   290

Repented all his sins, and made a last
   Irrevocable vow of reformation;
Nothing should tempt him more (this peril past)
   To quit his academic occupation
In cloisters of the classic Salamanca,   295
To follow Juan's wake like Sancho Panza.

38

But now there came a flash of hope once more:
   Day broke, and the wind lulled – the masts were gone,
The leak increased; shoals round her, but no shore,
   The vessel swam, yet still she held her own.   300
They tried the pumps again, and though before
   Their desperate efforts seemed all useless grown,
A glimpse of sunshine set some hands to bale –
The stronger pumped, the weaker thrummed a sail.

39

Under the vessel's keel the sail was past,   305
   And for the moment it had some effect;
But with a leak, and not a stick of mast,
   Nor rag of canvas, what could they expect?
But still 'tis best to struggle to the last,
   'Tis never too late to be wholly wrecked –   310
And though 'tis true that man can only die once,
'Tis not so pleasant in the Gulf of Lyons.

40

There winds and waves had hurled them, and from thence,
   Without their will, they carried them away;
For they were forced with steering to dispense,   315
   And never had as yet a quiet day
On which they might repose, or even commence
   A jury-mast or rudder, or could say
The ship would swim an hour, which, by good luck,
Still swam – though not exactly like a duck.   320

41

The wind, in fact, perhaps, was rather less,
   But the ship laboured so, they scarce could hope
To weather out much longer; the distress
   Was also great with which they had to cope
For want of water, and their solid mess   325
   Was scant enough: in vain the telescope
Was used – nor sail nor shore appeared in sight,
Nought but the heavy sea, and coming night.

42

Again the weather threatened; again blew
   A gale, and in the fore- and after-hold   330
Water appeared – yet, though the people knew
   All this, the most were patient, and some bold,
Until the chains and leathers were worn through
   Of all our pumps: a wreck complete she rolled
At mercy of the waves, whose mercies are   335
Like human beings during civil war.

43

Then came the carpenter at last, with tears
   In his rough eyes, and told the captain he
Could do no more; he was a man in years,
   And long had voyaged through many a stormy sea,   340
And if he wept at length, they were not fears
   That made his eyelids as a woman's be,
But he, poor fellow, had a wife and children,
Two things for dying people quite bewildering.

44

The ship was evidently settling now   345
   Fast by the head; and, all distinction gone,
Some went to prayers again, and made a vow
   Of candles to their saints – but there were none
To pay them with; and some looked o'er the bow;
   Some hoisted out the boats; and there was one   350
That begged Pedrillo for an absolution,
Who told him to be damned   in his confusion.

45

Some lashed them in their hammocks, some put on
   Their best clothes, as if going to a fair;
Some cursed the day on which they saw the sun,   355
   And gnashed their teeth and, howling, tore their hair;
And others went on as they had begun,
   Getting the boats out, being well aware
That a tight boat will live in a rough sea,
Unless with breakers close beneath her lee.   360

46

The worst of all was that, in their condition,
   Having been several days in great distress,
'Twas difficult to get out such provision
   As now might render their long suffering less –
Men, even when dying, dislike inanition.   365
   Their stock was damaged by the weather's stress:

Two casks of biscuit and a keg of butter
Were all that could be thrown into the cutter.

47

But in the longboat they contrived to stow
   Some pounds of bread, though injured by the wet;   370
Water, a twenty gallon cask or so;
   Six flasks of wine; and they contrived to get
A portion of their beef up from below,
   And with a piece of pork, moreover, met,
But scarce enough to serve them for a luncheon –   375
Then there was rum, eight gallons in a puncheon.

48

The other boats, the yawl and pinnace, had
   Been stove in the beginning of the gale;
And the longboat's condition was but bad,
   As there were but two blankets for a sail   380
And one oar for a mast, which a young lad
   Threw in by good luck over the ship's rail –
And two boats could not hold, far less be stored,
To save one half the people then on board.

49

'Twas twilight, and the sunless day went down   385
   Over the waste of waters, like a veil
Which, if withdrawn, would but disclose the frown
   Of one whose hate is masked but to assail;
Thus to their hopeless eyes the night was shown
   And grimly darkled o'er their faces pale,   390
And the dim desolate deep; twelve days had Fear
Been their familiar, and now Death was here.

50

Some trial had been making at a raft
   With little hope in such a rolling sea –
A sort of thing at which one would have laughed,   395
   If any laughter at such times could be,
Unless with people who too much have quaffed,
   And have a kind of wild and horrid glee,
Half-epileptical, and half-hysterical:
Their preservation would have been a miracle.   400

51

At half-past eight o'clock, booms, hencoops, spars,
   And all things, for a chance, had been cast loose,
That still could keep afloat the struggling tars –
   For yet they strove, although of no great use.

But the same cause, conductive to his loss,   450
Left him so drunk, he jumped into the wave
    As o'er the cutter's edge he tried to cross,
And so he found a wine-and-watery grave;
    They could not rescue him although so close,
Because the sea ran higher every minute,   455
And for the boat – the crew kept crowding in it.

58

A small old spaniel which had been Don Jóse's,
    His father's, whom he loved, as ye may think
(For on such things the memory reposes
    With tenderness), stood howling on the brink,   460
Knowing (dogs have such intellectual noses!),
    No doubt, the vessel was about to sink;
And Juan caught him up, and ere he stepped
Off, threw him in, then after him he leapt.

59

He also stuffed his money where he could   465
    About his person, and Pedrillo's too –
Who let him do, in fact, whate'er he would,
    Not knowing what himself to say or do,
As every rising wave his dread renewed;
    But Juan, trusting they might still get through,   470
And deeming there were remedies for any ill,
Thus re-embarked his tutor and his spaniel.

60

'Twas a rough night, and blew so stiffly yet,
    That the sail was becalmed between the seas,
Though on the wave's high top too much to set,   475
    They dared not take it in for all the breeze;

61

Nine souls more went in her: the longboat still
  Kept above water, with an oar for mast;
Two blankets stitched together, answering ill
  Instead of sail, were to the oar made fast –
Though every wave rolled menacing to fill,   485
  And present peril all before surpassed,
They grieved for those who perished with the cutter,
And also for the biscuit casks and butter.

62

The sun rose red and fiery, a sure sign
  Of the continuance of the gale: to run   490
Before the sea, until it should grow fine,
  Was all that for the present could be done.
A few teaspoonfuls of their rum and wine
  Was served out to the people, who begun
To faint, and damaged bread wet through the bags,   495
And most of them had little clothes but rags.

63

They counted thirty, crowded in a space
  Which left scarce room for motion or exertion.
They did their best to modify their case:
  One half sat up, though numbed with the immersion,   500
While t'other half were laid down in their place
  At watch and watch; thus, shivering like the tertian
Ague in its cold fit, they filled their boat,
With nothing but the sky for a greatcoat.

64

'Tis very certain the desire of life   505
  Prolongs it; this is obvious to physicians
When patients, neither plagued with friends nor wife,
  Survive through very desperate conditions,
Because they still can hope, nor shines the knife
  Nor shears of Atropos before their visions: 510
Despair of all recovery spoils longevity,
And makes men's miseries of alarming brevity.

65

'Tis said that persons living on annuities
  Are longer lived than others – God knows why,
Unless to plague the grantors; yet so true it is,   515
  That some, I really think, *do* never die.
Of any creditors the worst a Jew it is,
  And *that's* their mode of furnishing supply:

In my young days they lent me cash that way,
Which I found very troublesome to pay.   520

66

'Tis thus with people in an open boat,
    They live upon the love of life, and bear
More than can be believed, or even thought,
    And stand like rocks the tempest's wear and tear;
And hardship still has been the sailor's lot   525
    Since Noah's ark went cruising here and there;
She had a curious crew as well as cargo,
Like the first old Greek privateer, the Argo.

67

But man is a carnivorous production
    And must have meals, at least one meal a day;   530
He cannot live, like woodcocks, upon suction,
    But, like the shark and tiger, must have prey –
Although his anatomical construction
    Bears vegetables in a grumbling way,
Your labouring people think beyond all question   535
Beef, veal, and mutton, better for digestion.

68

And thus it was with this our hapless crew,
    For on the third day there came on a calm,
And though at first their strength it might renew,
    And lying on their weariness like balm,   540
Lulled them like turtles sleeping on the blue
    Of ocean, when they woke they felt a qualm,
And fell all ravenously on their provision,
Instead of hoarding it with due precision.

69

The consequence was easily foreseen: 545
    They ate up all they had, and drank their wine
In spite of all remonstrances, and then –
    On what, in fact, next day were they to dine?
They hoped the wind would rise, these foolish men,
    And carry them to shore! These hopes were fine,   550
But as they had but one oar, and that brittle,
It would have been more wise to save their victual.

70

The fourth day came, but not a breath of air,
    And ocean slumbered like an unweaned child;

The fifth day, and their boat lay floating there,   555
   The sea and sky were blue, and clear, and mild –
With their one oar (I wish they had had a pair)
   What could they do? And hunger's rage grew wild;
So Juan's spaniel, spite of his entreating,
Was killed, and portioned out for present eating.   560

71
On the sixth day they fed upon his hide,
   And Juan, who had still refused, because
The creature was his father's dog that died,
   Now feeling all the vulture in his jaws,
With some remorse received (though first denied)   565
   As a great favour one of the forepaws,
Which he divided with Pedrillo, who
Devoured it, longing for the other too.

72
The seventh day, and no wind; the burning sun
   Blistered and scorched, and, stagnant on the sea,   570
They lay like carcasses; and hope was none,
   Save in the breeze that came not. Savagely
They glared upon each other – all was done,
   Water, and wine, and food; and you might see
The longings of the cannibal arise   575
(Although they spoke not) in their wolfish eyes.

73
At length one whispered his companion, who
   Whispered another, and thus it went round,
And then into a hoarser murmur grew –
   An ominous, and wild, and desperate sound;   580
And when his comrade's thought each sufferer knew,
   'Twas but his own, suppressed till now, he found.
And out they spoke of lots for flesh and blood,
And who should die to be his fellow's food.

74
But ere they came to this, they that day shared   585
   Some leathern caps, and what remained of shoes;
And then they looked around them and despaired,
   And none to be the sacrifice would choose;
At length the lots were torn up and prepared,
   But of materials that much shock the muse –   590
Having no paper, for the want of better,
They took by force from Juan Julia's letter.

75

The lots were made, and marked, and mixed and handed
   In silent horror, and their distribution
Lulled even the savage hunger which demanded,   595
   Like the Promethean vulture, this pollution;
None in particular had sought or planned it,
   'Twas nature gnawed them to this resolution
By which none were permitted to be neuter –
And the lot fell on Juan's luckless tutor.   600

76

He but requested to be bled to death:
   The surgeon had his instruments, and bled
Pedrillo, and so gently ebbed his breath,
   You hardly could perceive when he was dead.
He died as born, a Catholic in faith,   605
   Like most in the belief in which they're bred,
And first a little crucifix he kissed,
And then held out his jugular and wrist.

77

The surgeon, as there was no other fee,
   Had his first choice of morsels for his pains;   610
But being thirstiest at the moment, he
   Preferred a draught from the fast-flowing veins:
Part was divided, part thrown in the sea,
   And such things as the entrails and the brains
Regaled two sharks, who followed o'er the billow –   615
The sailors ate the rest of poor Pedrillo.

78

The sailors ate him, all save three or four
   Who were not quite so fond of animal food;
To these was added Juan who, before
   Refusing his own spaniel, hardly could   620
Feel now his appetite increased much more;
   'Twas not to be expected that he should,
Even in extremity of their disaster,
Dine with them on his pastor and his master.

79

'Twas better that he did not, for, in fact,   625
   The consequence was awful in the extreme;
For they who were most ravenous in the act
   Went raging mad – Lord, how they did blaspheme,
And foam and roll, with strange convulsions racked,
   Drinking salt-water like a mountain-stream,   630

Tearing and grinning, howling, screeching, swearing,
And, with hyena laughter, died despairing.

80

Their numbers were much thinned by this infliction,
   And all the rest were thin enough, Heaven knows;
And some of them had lost their recollection,   635
   Happier than they who still perceived their woes;
But others pondered on a new dissection,
   As if not warned sufficiently by those
Who had already perished, suffering madly,
For having used their appetites so sadly.   640

81

And next they thought upon the master's mate
   As fattest – but he saved himself because,
Besides being much averse from such a fate,
   There were some other reasons: the first was
He had been rather indisposed of late;   645
   And that which chiefly proved his saving clause
Was a small present made to him at Cadiz,
By general subscription of the ladies.

82

Of poor Pedrillo something still remained,
   But was used sparingly – some were afraid,   650
And others still their appetites constrained,
   Or but at times a little supper made;
All except Juan, who throughout abstained,
   Chewing a piece of bamboo, and some lead:
At length they caught two boobies and a noddy,   655
And then they left off eating the dead body.

83

And if Pedrillo's fate should shocking be,
   Remember Ugolino condescends
To eat the head of his arch enemy
   The moment after he politely ends   660
His tale; if foes be food in hell, at sea
   'Tis surely fair to dine upon our friends
When shipwreck's short allowance grows too scanty,
Without being much more horrible than Dante.

84

And the same night there fell a shower of rain   665
   For which their mouths gaped, like the cracks of earth
When dried to summer dust; till taught by pain,
   Men really know not what good water's worth:

If you had been in Turkey or in Spain,
   Or with a famished boat's-crew had your berth,   670
Or in the desert heard the camel's bell,
You'd wish yourself where Truth is – in a well.

85

It poured down torrents, but they were no richer
   Until they found a ragged piece of sheet
Which served them as a sort of spongy pitcher,   675
   And when they deemed its moisture was complete,
They wrung it out, and though a thirsty ditcher
   Might not have thought the scanty draught so sweet
As a full pot of porter, to their thinking
They ne'er till now had known the joys of drinking.   680

86

And their baked lips, with many a bloody crack,
   Sucked in the moisture, which like nectar streamed;
Their throats were ovens, their swoln tongues were black
   As the rich man's in hell, who vainly screamed
To beg the beggar, who could not rain back   685
   A drop of dew, when every drop had seemed
To taste of heaven (if this be true, indeed,
Some Christians have a comfortable creed).

87

There were two fathers in this ghastly crew,
   And with them their two sons, of whom the one   690
Was more robust and hardy to the view,
   But he died early; and when he was gone,
His nearest messmate told his sire, who threw
   One glance on him, and said, 'Heaven's will be done!
I can do nothing', and he saw him thrown   695
Into the deep without a tear or groan.

88

The other father had a weaklier child,
   Of a soft cheek, and aspect delicate;
But the boy bore up long, and with a mild
   And patient spirit held aloof his fate;   700
Little he said, and now and then he smiled,
   As if to win a part from off the weight
He saw increasing on his father's heart,
With the deep deadly thought that they must part.

89

And o'er him bent his sire, and never raised   705
   His eyes from off his face, but wiped the foam

From his pale lips, and ever on him gazed,
    And when the wished-for shower at length was come,
And the boy's eyes, which the dull film half glazed,
    Brightened, and for a moment seemed to roam,   710
He squeezed from out a rag some drops of rain
Into his dying child's mouth – but in vain.

90

The boy expired; the father held the clay,
    And looked upon it long, and when at last
Death left no doubt, and the dead burden lay   715
    Stiff on his heart, and pulse and hope were past,
He watched it wistfully, until away
    'Twas borne by the rude wave wherein 'twas cast.
Then he himself sunk down all dumb and shivering,
And gave no sign of life, save his limbs quivering.   720

91

Now overhead a rainbow, bursting through
    The scattering clouds, shone, spanning the dark sea,
Resting its bright base on the quivering blue;
    And all within its arch appeared to be
Clearer than that without, and its wide hue   725
    Waxed broad and waving, like a banner free,
Then changed like to a bow that's bent, and then
Forsook the dim eyes of these shipwrecked men.

92

It changed, of course; a heavenly chameleon,
    The airy child of vapour and the sun,   730
Brought forth in purple, cradled in vermilion,
    Baptized in molten gold, and swathed in dun,
Glittering like crescents o'er a Turk's pavilion,
    And blending every colour into one,
Just like a black eye in a recent scuffle   735
(For sometimes we must box without the muffle).

93

Our shipwrecked seamen thought it a good omen –
    It is as well to think so, now and then;
'Twas an old custom of the Greek and Roman,
    And may become of great advantage when   740
Folks are discouraged; and most surely no men
    Had greater need to nerve themselves again
Than these, and so this rainbow looked like hope –
Quite a celestial kaleidoscope.

94

About this time a beautiful white bird,   745
   Webfooted, not unlike a dove in size
And plumage (probably it might have erred
   Upon its course), passed oft before their eyes
And tried to perch, although it saw and heard
   The men within the boat, and in this guise   750
It came and went, and fluttered round them till
Night fell – this seemed a better omen still.

95

But in this case I also must remark
   'Twas well this bird of promise did not perch,
Because the tackle of our shattered bark   755
   Was not so safe for roosting as a church;
And had it been the dove from Noah's ark,
   Returning there from her successful search,
Which in their way that moment chanced to fall,
They would have eat her, olive-branch and all.   760

96

With twilight it again came on to blow,
   But not with violence; the stars shone out,
The boat made way; yet now they were so low,
   They knew not where nor what they were about;
Some fancied they saw land, and some said 'No!'   765
   The frequent fog-banks gave them cause to doubt –
Some swore that they heard breakers, others guns,
And all mistook about the latter once.

97

As morning broke the light wind died away,
   When he who had the watch sung out and swore   770
If 'twas not land that rose with the sun's ray,
   He wished that land he never might see more;
And the rest rubbed their eyes, and saw a bay,
   Or thought they saw, and shaped their course for shore –
For shore it was, and gradually grew   775
Distinct, and high, and palpable to view.

98

And then of these some part burst into tears,
   And others, looking with a stupid stare,
Could not yet separate their hopes from fears,
   And seemed as if they had no further care;   780
While a few prayed (the first time for some years),
   And at the bottom of the boat three were

Asleep; they shook them by the hand and head,
And tried to awaken them, but found them dead.

99

The day before, fast sleeping on the water,   785
   They found a turtle of the hawk's-bill kind,
And by good fortune gliding softly, caught her,
   Which yielded a day's life, and to their mind
Proved even still a more nutritious matter
   Because it left encouragement behind: 790
They thought that in such perils, more than chance
Had sent them this for their deliverance.

100

The land appeared a high and rocky coast,
   And higher grew the mountains as they drew,
Set by a current, toward it: they were lost   795
   In various conjectures, for none knew
To what part of the earth they had been tossed,
   So changeable had been the winds that blew;
Some thought it was Mount Etna, some the highlands
Of Candia, Cyprus, Rhodes, or other islands.   800

101

Meantime the current, with a rising gale,
   Still set them onwards to the welcome shore
Like Charon's bark of spectres, dull and pale.
   Their living freight was now reduced to four,
And three dead, whom their strength could not avail   805
   To heave into the deep with those before –
Though the two sharks still followed them, and dashed
The spray into their faces as they splashed.

102

Famine, despair, cold, thirst and heat, had done
   Their work on them by turns, and thinned them to   810
Such things a mother had not known her son
   Amidst the skeletons of that gaunt crew;
By night chilled, by day scorched – thus one by one
   They perished, until withered to these few,
But chiefly by a species of self-slaughter,   815
In washing down Pedrillo with salt water.

103

As they drew nigh the land, which now was seen
   Unequal in its aspect here and there,
They felt the freshness of its growing green
   That waved in forest-tops and smoothed the air,   820

And fell upon their glazed eyes like a screen
    From glistening waves, and skies so hot and bare –
Lovely seemed any object that should sweep
Away the vast, salt, dread, eternal deep.

104

The shore looked wild, without a trace of man,   825
    And girt by formidable waves; but they
Were mad for land, and thus their course they ran,
    Though right ahead the roaring breakers lay:
A reef between them also now began
    To show its boiling surf and bounding spray –   830
But finding no place for their landing better,
They ran the boat for shore, and overset her.

105

But in his native stream, the Guadalquivir,
    Juan to lave his youthful limbs was wont;
And having learnt to swim in that sweet river,   835
    Had often turned the art to some account:
A better swimmer you could scarce see ever,
    He could, perhaps, have passed the Hellespont,
As once (a feat on which ourselves we prided)
Leander, Mr Ekenhead, and I did.   840

106

So here, though faint, emaciated, and stark,
    He buoyed his boyish limbs, and strove to ply
With the quick wave, and gain, ere it was dark,
    The beach which lay before him, high and dry:
The greatest danger here was from a shark   845
    That carried off his neighbour by the thigh;
As for the other two they could not swim,
So nobody arrived on shore but him.

107

Nor yet had he arrived but for the oar,
    Which, providentially for him, was washed   850
Just as his feeble arms could strike no more,
    And the hard wave o'erwhelmed him as 'twas dashed
Within his grasp; he clung to it, and sore
    The waters beat while he thereto was lashed;
At last, with swimming, wading, scrambling, he   855
Rolled on the beach, half-senseless, from the sea.

108

There, breathless, with his digging nails he clung
    Fast to the sand, lest the returning wave,

From whose reluctant roar his life he wrung,
   Should suck him back to her insatiate grave: 860
And there he lay, full-length, where he was flung,
   Before the entrance of a cliff-worn cave,
With just enough of life to feel its pain,
And deem that it was saved, perhaps, in vain.

109

With slow and staggering effort he arose,   865
   But sunk again upon his bleeding knee
And quivering hand; and then he looked for those
   Who long had been his mates upon the sea,
But none of them appeared to share his woes
   Save one, a corpse from out the famished three,   870
Who died two days before, and now had found
An unknown barren beach for burial ground.

110

And as he gazed, his dizzy brain spun fast,
   And down he sunk; and as he sunk, the sand
Swam round and round, and all his senses passed: 875
   He fell upon his side, and his stretched hand
Drooped dripping on the oar (their jury-mast),
   And, like a withered lily, on the land
His slender frame and pallid aspect lay,
As fair a thing as e'er was formed of clay.   880

111

How long in his damp trance young Juan lay
   He knew not, for the earth was gone for him,
And Time had nothing more of night nor day
   For his congealing blood, and senses dim;
And how this heavy faintness passed away   885
   He knew not, till each painful pulse and limb
And tingling vein seemed throbbing back to life –
For Death, though vanquished, still retired with strife.

112

His eyes he opened, shut, again unclosed,
   For all was doubt and dizziness; methought   890
He still was in the boat, and had but dozed,
   And felt again with his despair o'erwrought,
And wished it death in which he had reposed,
   And then once more his feelings back were brought;
And slowly by his swimming eyes was seen   895
A lovely female face of seventeen.

113

'Twas bending close o'er his, and the small mouth
   Seemed almost prying into his for breath;
And chafing him, the soft warm hand of youth
   Recalled his answering spirits back from death;   900
And, bathing his chill temples, tried to soothe
   Each pulse to animation, till beneath
Its gentle touch and trembling care, a sigh
To these kind efforts made a low reply.

114

Then was the cordial poured, and mantle flung   905
   Around his scarce-clad limbs; and the fair arm
Raised higher the faint head which o'er it hung;
   And her transparent cheek, all pure and warm,
Pillowed his death-like forehead; then she wrung
   His dewy curls, long drenched by every storm;   910
And watched with eagerness each throb that drew
A sigh from his heaved bosom – and hers too.

115

And lifting him with care into the cave,
   The gentle girl, and her attendant – one
Young, yet her elder, and of brow less grave,   915
   And more robust of figure – then begun
To kindle fire, and as the new flames gave
   Light to the rocks that roofed them, which the sun
Had never seen, the maid, or whatsoe'er
She was, appeared distinct, and tall, and fair.   920

116

Her brow was overhung with coins of gold
   That sparkled o'er the auburn of her hair,
Her clustering hair, whose longer locks were rolled
   In braids behind, and though her stature were
Even of the highest for a female mould,   925
   They nearly reached her heel; and in her air
There was a something which bespoke command,
As one who was a lady in the land.

117

Her hair, I said, was auburn; but her eyes
   Were black as death, their lashes the same hue,   930
Of downcast length, in whose silk shadow lies
   Deepest attraction – for when to the view
Forth from its raven fringe the full glance flies,
   Ne'er with such force the swiftest arrow flew;

'Tis as the snake late coiled, who pours his length,   935
And hurls at once his venom and his strength.

118

Her brow was white and low, her cheek's pure dye
   Like twilight rosy still with the set sun;
Short upper lip, sweet lips! – that make us sigh
   Ever to have seen such, for she was one   940
Fit for the model of a statuary
   (A race of mere impostors, when all's done;
I've seen much finer women, ripe and real,
Than all the nonsense of their stone ideal).

119

I'll tell you why I say so, for 'tis just   945
   One should not rail without a decent cause:
There was an Irish lady, to whose bust
   I ne'er saw justice done, and yet she was
A frequent model; and if e'er she must
   Yield to stern Time and Nature's wrinkling laws,   950
They will destroy a face which mortal thought
Ne'er compassed, nor less mortal chisel wrought.

120

And such was she, the lady of the cave:
   Her dress was very different from the Spanish –
Simpler, and yet of colours not so grave;   955
   For, as you know, the Spanish women banish
Bright hues when out of doors, and yet, while wave
   Around them (what I hope will never vanish)
The basquiña and the mantilla, they
Seem at the same time mystical and gay.   960

121

But with our damsel this was not the case:
   Her dress was many-coloured, finely spun;
Her locks curled negligently round her face,
   But through them gold and gems profusely shone;
Her girdle sparkled, and the richest lace   965
   Flowed in her veil, and many a precious stone
Flashed on her little hand; but, what was shocking,
Her small snow feet had slippers, but no stocking.

122

The other female's dress was not unlike,
   But of inferior materials; she   970
Had not so many ornaments to strike –
   Her hair had silver only, bound to be

Her dowry; and her veil, in form alike,
    Was coarser; and her air, though firm, less free;
Her hair was thicker, but less long; her eyes   975
As black, but quicker, and of smaller size.

123

And these two tended him, and cheered him both
    With food and raiment, and those soft attentions
Which are (as I must own) of female growth,
    And have ten thousand delicate inventions: 980
They made a most superior mess of broth,
    A thing which poesy but seldom mentions,
But the best dish that e'er was cooked since Homer's
Achilles ordered dinner for newcomers.

124

I'll tell you who they were, this female pair,   985
    Lest they should seem princesses in disguise;
Besides, I hate all mystery, and that air
    Of claptrap, which your recent poets prize;
And so, in short, the girls they really were
    They shall appear before your curious eyes –   990
Mistress and maid; the first was only daughter
Of an old man, who lived upon the water.

125

A fisherman he had been in his youth,
    And still a sort of fisherman was he;
But other speculations were, in sooth,   995
    Added to his connection with the sea –
Perhaps not so respectable, in truth:
    A little smuggling, and some piracy
Left him, at last, the sole of many masters
Of an ill-gotten million of piastres.   1000

126

A fisher, therefore, was he – though of men,
    Like Peter the Apostle – and he fished
For wandering merchant vessels, now and then,
    And sometimes caught as many as he wished;
The cargoes he confiscated, and gain   1005
    He sought in the slave-market too, and dished
Full many a morsel for that Turkish trade,
By which, no doubt, a good deal may be made.

127

He was a Greek, and on his isle had built
    (One of the wild and smaller Cyclades)   1010

A very handsome house from out his guilt,
 And there he lived exceedingly at ease;
Heaven knows what cash he got, or blood he spilt –
 A sad old fellow was he, if you please,
But this I know: it was a spacious building,   1015
Full of barbaric carving, paint, and gilding.

128

He had an only daughter called Haidee,
 The greatest heiress of the Eastern Isles;
Besides, so very beautiful was she,
 Her dowry was as nothing to her smiles: 1020
Still in her teens, and like a lovely tree
 She grew to womanhood, and between whiles
Rejected several suitors, just to learn
How to accept a better in his turn.

129

And walking out upon the beach below   1025
 The cliff, towards sunset, on that day she found,
Insensible – not dead, but nearly so –
 Don Juan, almost famished, and half-drowned;
But being naked, she was shocked, you know,
 Yet deemed herself in common pity bound,   1030
As far as in her lay, 'to take him in,
A stranger', dying, with so white a skin.

130

But taking him into her father's house
 Was not exactly the best way to save,
But like conveying to the cat the mouse,   1035
 Or people in a trance into their grave;
Because the good old man had so much νους,
 Unlike the honest Arab thieves so brave,
He would have hospitably cured the stranger,
And sold him instantly when out of danger.   1040

131

And therefore, with her maid, she thought it best
 (A virgin always on her maid relies)
To place him in the cave for present rest;
 And when, at last, he opened his black eyes,
Their charity increased about their guest,   1045
 And their compassion grew to such a size,
It opened half the turnpike-gates to heaven
(St Paul says 'tis the toll which must be given).

132

They made a fire, but such a fire as they
 Upon the moment could contrive with such   1050
Materials as were cast up round the bay –
 Some broken planks, and oars, that to the touch
Were nearly tinder, since so long they lay,
 A mast was almost crumbled to a crutch;
But, by God's grace, here wrecks were in such plenty,   1055
That there was fuel to have furnished twenty.

133

He had a bed of furs, and a pelisse,
 For Haidee stripped her sables off to make
His couch; and, that he might be more at ease
 And warm, in case by chance he should awake,   1060
They also gave a petticoat apiece,
 She and her maid, and promised by daybreak
To pay him a fresh visit, with a dish
For breakfast, of eggs, coffee, bread, and fish.

134

And thus they left him to his lone repose.   1065
 Juan slept like a top, or like the dead
Who sleep at last, perhaps (God only knows),
 Just for the present; and in his lulled head
Not even a vision of his former woes
 Throbbed in accursed dreams, which sometimes spread   1070
Unwelcome visions of our former years,
Till the eye, cheated, opens thick with tears.

135

Young Juan slept all dreamless, but the maid
 Who smoothed his pillow as she left the den
Looked back upon him, and a moment stayed,   1075
 And turned, believing that he called again.
He slumbered; yet she thought, at least she said
 (The heart will slip even as the tongue and pen),
He had pronounced her name – but she forgot
That at this moment Juan knew it not.   1080

136

And pensive to her father's house she went,
 Enjoining silence strict to Zoe, who
Better than her knew what, in fact, she meant,
 She being wiser by a year or two:
A year or two's an age when rightly spent,   1085
 And Zoe spent hers, as most women do,

In gaining all that useful sort of knowledge
Which is acquired in nature's good old college.

137

The morn broke, and found Juan slumbering still
    Fast in his cave, and nothing clashed upon   1090
His rest; the rushing of the neighbouring rill
    And the young beams of the excluded sun
Troubled him not, and he might sleep his fill;
    And need he had of slumber yet, for none
Had suffered more – his hardships were comparative   1095
To those related in my granddad's *Narrative.*

138

Not so Haidee: she sadly tossed and tumbled,
    And started from her sleep, and, turning o'er,
Dreamed of a thousand wrecks o'er which she stumbled,
    And handsome corpses strewed upon the shore;   1100
And woke her maid so early that she grumbled,
    And called her father's old slaves up, who swore
In several oaths – Armenian, Turk, and Greek;
They knew not what to think of such a freak.

139

But up she got, and up she made them get   1105
    With some pretence about the sun, that makes
Sweet skies just when he rises, or is set;
    And 'tis, no doubt, a sight to see when breaks
Bright Phoebus, while the mountains still are wet
    With mist, and every bird with him awakes,   1110
And night is flung off like a mourning suit
Worn for a husband, or some other brute.

140

I say, the sun is a most glorious sight;
    I've seen him rise full oft, indeed of late
I have sat up on purpose all the night,   1115
    Which hastens, as physicians say, one's fate –
And so all ye, who would be in the right
    In health and purse, begin your day to date
From daybreak, and when coffined at fourscore,
Engrave upon the plate, you rose at four.   1120

141

And Haidee met the morning face to face;
    Her own was freshest, though a feverish flush
Had dyed it with the headlong blood, whose race
    From heart to cheek is curbed into a blush,

Like to a torrent which a mountain's base,   1125
    That overpowers some alpine river's rush,
Checks to a lake, whose waves in circles spread,
Or the Red Sea – but the sea is not red.

142

And down the cliff the island virgin came,
    And near the cave her quick light footsteps drew,   1130
While the sun smiled on her with his first flame,
    And young Aurora kissed her lips with dew,
Taking her for a sister; just the same
    Mistake you would have made on seeing the two,
Although the mortal, quite as fresh and fair,   1135
Had all the advantage too of not being air.

143

And when into the cavern Haidee stepped
    All timidly, yet rapidly, she saw
That like an infant Juan sweetly slept;
    And then she stopped, and stood as if in awe   1140
(For sleep is awful), and on tiptoe crept
    And wrapped him closer, lest the air, too raw,
Should reach his blood, then o'er him still as death
Bent, with hushed lips, that drank his scarce-drawn breath.

144

And thus like to an angel o'er the dying   1145
    Who die in righteousness, she leaned; and there
All tranquilly the shipwrecked boy was lying,
    As o'er him lay the calm and stirless air.
But Zoe the meantime some eggs was frying,
    Since, after all, no doubt the youthful pair   1150
Must breakfast, and betimes; lest they should ask it,
She drew out her provision from the basket.

145

She knew that the best feelings must have victual
    And that a shipwrecked youth would hungry be;
Besides, being less in love, she yawned a little,   1155
    And felt her veins chilled by the neighbouring sea.
And so she cooked their breakfast to a tittle;
    I can't say that she gave them any tea,
But there were eggs, fruit, coffee, bread, fish, honey,
With Scio wine – and all for love, not money.   1160

146

And Zoe, when the eggs were ready, and
    The coffee made, would fain have wakened Juan,

But Haidee stopped her with her quick small hand,
   And without a word, a sign her finger drew on
Her lip, which Zoe needs must understand;   1165
   And, the first breakfast spoilt, prepared a new one,
Because her mistress would not let her break
That sleep which seemed as it would ne'er awake.

147

For still he lay, and on his thing worn cheek
   A purple hectic played like dying day   1170
On the snow-tops of distant hills; the streak
   Of sufferance yet upon his forehead lay,
Where the blue veins looked shadowy, shrunk, and weak;
   And his black curls were dewy with the spray
Which weighed upon them yet, all damp and salt,   1175
Mixed with the stony vapours of the vault.

148

And she bent o'er him, and he lay beneath,
   Hushed as the babe upon its mother's breast,
Drooped as the willow when no winds can breathe,
   Lulled like the depth of ocean when at rest,   1180
Fair as the crowning rose of the whole wreath,
   Soft as the callow cygnet in its rest;
In short, he was a very pretty fellow,
Although his woes had turned him rather yellow.

149

He woke and gazed, and would have slept again,   1185
   But the fair face which met his eyes forbade
Those eyes to close, though weariness and pain
   Had further sleep a further pleasure made;
For woman's face was never formed in vain
   For Juan, so that, even when he prayed,   1190
He turned from grisly saints and martyrs hairy
To the sweet portraits of the Virgin Mary.

150

And thus upon his elbow he arose,
   And looked upon the lady, in whose cheek
The pale contended with the purple rose,   1195
   As with an effort she began to speak;
Her eyes were eloquent, her words would pose,
   Although she told him, in good modern Greek,
With an Ionian accent, low and sweet,
That he was faint, and must not talk, but eat.   1200

151

Now Juan could not understand a word,
   Being no Grecian; but he had an ear,
And her voice was the warble of a bird,
   So soft, so sweet, so delicately clear,
That finer, simpler music ne'er was heard;   1205
   The sort of sound we echo with a tear
Without knowing why – an overpowering tone
Whence melody descends as from a throne.

152

And Juan gazed as one who is awoke
   By a distant organ, doubting if he be   1210
Not yet a dreamer, till the spell is broke
   By the watchman, or some such reality,
Or by one's early valet's cursed knock –
   At least it is a heavy sound to me
Who like a morning slumber, for the night   1215
Shows stars and women in a better light.

153

And Juan, too, was helped out from his dream
   Or sleep, or whatsoe'er it was, by feeling
A most prodigious appetite: the stream
   Of Zoe's cookery no doubt was stealing   1220
Upon his senses, and the kindling beam
   Of the new fire, which Zoe kept up, kneeling,
To stir her viands, made him quite awake
And long for food, but chiefly a beefsteak.

154

But beef is rare within these oxless isles;   1225
   Goat's flesh there is, no doubt, and kid, and mutton;
And, when a holiday upon them smiles,
   A joint upon their barbarous spits they put on:
But this occurs but seldom, between whiles,
   For some of these are rocks with scarce a hut on;   1230
Others are fair and fertile, among which
This, though not large, was one of the most rich.

155

I say that beef is rare, and can't help thinking
   That the old fable of the Minotaur –
From which our modern morals, rightly shrinking,   1235
   Condemn the royal lady's taste who wore
A cow's shape for a mask – was only (sinking
   The allegory) a mere type, no more;

That Pasiphae promoted breeding cattle
To make the Cretans bloodier in battle.   1240

156

For we all know that English people are
  Fed upon beef (I won't say much of beer
Because 'tis liquor only, and being far
  From this my subject, has no business here);
We know, too, they are very fond of war,   1245
  A pleasure (like all pleasures) rather dear;
So were the Cretans – from which I infer
That beef and battles both were owing to her.

157

But to resume. The languid Juan raised
  His head upon his elbow, and he saw   1250
A sight on which he had not lately gazed,
  As all his latter meals had been quite raw –
Three or four things, for which the Lord he praised,
  And, feeling still the famished vulture gnaw,
He fell upon whate'er was offered, like   1255
A priest, a shark, an alderman, or pike.

158

He ate, and he was well supplied; and she
  Who watched him like a mother, would have fed
Him past all bounds, because she smiled to see
  Such an appetite in one she had deemed dead: 1260
But Zoe, being older than Haidee,
  Knew (by tradition, for she ne'er had read)
That famished people must be slowly nursed,
And fed by spoonfuls, else they always burst.

159

And so she took the liberty to state,   1265
  Rather by deeds than words, because the case
Was urgent, that the gentleman whose fate
  Had made her mistress quit her bed to trace
The seashore at this hour, must leave his plate
  Unless he wished to die upon the place –   1270
She snatched it and refused another morsel,
Saying he had gorged enough to make a horse ill.

160

Next they – he being naked, save a tattered
  Pair of scarce decent trousers – went to work,
And in the fire his recent rags they scattered   1275
  And dressed him, for the present, like a Turk

Or Greek; that is (although it not much mattered),
   Omitting turban, slippers, pistols, dirk,
They furnished him, entire except some stitches,
With a clean shirt and very spacious breeches.   1280

161

And then fair Haidee tried her tongue at speaking,
   But not a word could Juan comprehend,
Although he listened so that the young Greek in
   Her earnestness would ne'er have made an end;
And, as he interrupted not, went ekeing   1285
   Her speech out to her protégée and friend,
Till pausing at the last her breath to take,
She saw he did not understand Romaic.

162

And then she had recourse to nods and signs,
   And smiles, and sparkles of the speaking eye,   1290
And read (the only book she could) the lines
   Of his fair face, and found, by sympathy,
The answer eloquent, where the soul shines
   And darts in one quick glance a long reply;
And thus in every look she saw expressed   1295
A world of words, and things at which she guessed.

163

And now, by dint of fingers and of eyes,
   And words repeated after her, he took
A lesson in her tongue – but by surmise,
   No doubt, less of her language than her look;   1300
As he who studies fervently the skies
   Turns oftener to the stars than to his book,
Thus Juan learned his alpha beta better
From Haidee's glance than any graven letter.

164

'Tis pleasing to be schooled in a strange tongue   1305
   By female lips and eyes; that is, I mean,
When both the teacher and the taught are young,
   As was the case, at least, where I have been;
They smile so when one's right, and when one's wrong
   They smile still more, and then there intervene   1310
Pressure of hands, perhaps even a chaste kiss;
I learned the little that I know by this –

165

That is, some words of Spanish, Turk, and Greek,
   Italian not at all, having no teachers;

Much English I cannot pretend to speak,   1315
   Learning that language chiefly from its preachers,
Barrow, South, Tillotson, whom every week
   I study, also Blair – the highest reachers
Of eloquence in piety and prose;
I hate your poets, so read none of those.   1320

166

As for the ladies, I have nought to say,
   A wanderer from the British world of fashion,
Where I, like other 'dogs, have had my day';
   Like other men too, may have had my passion –
But that, like other things, has passed away,   1325
   And all her fools whom I *could* lay the lash on:
Foes, friends, men, women, now are nought to me
But dreams of what has been, no more to be.

167

Return we to Don Juan. He begun
   To hear new words, and to repeat them, but   1330
Some feelings, universal as the sun,
   Were such as could not in his breast be shut
More than within the bosom of a nun;
   He was in love – as you would be, no doubt,
With a young benefactress; so was she,   1335
Just in the way we very often see.

168

And every day by daybreak   rather early
   For Juan, who was somewhat fond of rest,
She came into the cave, but it was merely
   To see her bird reposing in his nest;   1340
And she would softly stir his locks so curly,
   Without disturbing her yet-slumbering guest,
Breathing all gently o'er his cheek and mouth,
As o'er a bed of roses the sweet south.

169

And every morn his colour freshlier came,   1345
   And every day helped on his convalescence;
'Twas well, because health in the human frame
   Is pleasant, besides being true love's essence;
For health and idleness to passion's flame
   Are oil and gunpowder, and some good lessons   1350
Are also learnt from Ceres and from Bacchus,
Without whom Venus will not long attack us.

170

While Venus fills the heart (without heart really
   Love, though good always, is not quite so good),
Ceres presents a plate of vermicelli;   1355
   For love must be sustained like flesh and blood,
While Bacchus pours out wine, or hands a jelly.
   Eggs, oysters too, are amatory food;
But who is their purveyor from above
Heaven knows – it may be Neptune, Pan, or Jove.   1360

171

When Juan woke he found some good things ready;
   A bath, a breakfast, and the finest eyes
That ever made a youthful heart less steady,
   Besides her maid's, as pretty for their size –
But I have spoken of all this already,   1365
   And repetition's tiresome and unwise;
Well, Juan, after bathing in the sea,
Came always back to coffee and Haidee.

172

Both were so young, and one so innocent,
   That bathing passed for nothing; Juan seemed   1370
To her, as 'twere, the kind of being sent,
   Of whom these two years she had nightly dreamed:
A something to be loved, a creature meant
   To be her happiness, and whom she deemed
To render happy; all who joy would win   1375
Must share it – Happiness was born a twin.

173

It was such pleasure to behold him, such
   Enlargement of existence to partake
Nature with him, to thrill beneath his touch,
   To watch him slumbering, and to see him wake: 1380
To live with him for ever were too much,
   But then the thought of parting made her quake;
He was her own, her ocean-treasure, cast
Like a rich wreck – her first love, and her last.

174

And thus a moon rolled on, and fair Haidee   1385
   Paid daily visits to her boy, and took
Such plentiful precautions, that still he
   Remained unknown within his craggy nook;
At last her father's prows put out to sea,
   For certain merchantmen upon the look,   1390

Not as of yore to carry off an Io,
But three Ragusan vessels, bound for Scio.

175

Then came her freedom, for she had no mother,
   So that, her father being at sea, she was
Free as a married woman, or such other   1395
   Female, as where she likes may freely pass,
Without even the encumbrance of a brother –
   The freest she that ever gazed on glass
(I speak of Christian lands in this comparison,
Where wives, at least, are seldom kept in garrison).   1400

176

Now she prolonged her visits and her talk
   (For they must talk), and he had learnt to say
So much as to propose to take a walk –
   For little had he wandered since the day
On which, like a young flower snapped from the stalk,   1405
   Drooping and dewy on the beach he lay;
And thus they walked out in the afternoon,
And saw the sun set opposite the moon.

177

It was a wild and breaker-beaten coast,
   With cliffs above, and a broad sandy shore   1410
Guarded by shoals and rocks as by an host,
   With here and there a creek whose aspect wore
A better welcome to the tempest-tossed;
   And rarely ceased the haughty billow's roar,
Save on the dead long summer days, which make   1415
The outstretched ocean glitter like a lake.

178

And the small ripple spilt upon the beach
   Scarcely o'erpassed the cream of your champagne,
When o'er the brim the sparkling bumpers reach,
   That spring-dew of the spirit, the heart's rain!   1420
Few things surpass old wine – and they may preach
   Who please (the more because they preach in vain) –
Let us have wine and woman, mirth and laughter,
Sermons and soda-water the day after.

179

Man, being reasonable, must get drunk;   1425
   The best of life is but intoxication:
Glory, the grape, love, gold – in these are sunk
   The hopes of all men, and of every nation;

Without their sap, how branchless were the trunk
  Of life's strange tree, so fruitful on occasion.   1430
But to return; get very drunk, and when
You wake with headache, you shall see what then.

180

Ring for your valet, bid him quickly bring
  Some hock and soda-water – then you'll know
A pleasure worthy Xerxes the great king;   1435
  For not the blessed sherbet, sublimed with snow,
Nor the first sparkle of the desert-spring,
  Nor Burgundy in all its sunset glow,
After long travel, ennui, love, or slaughter,
Vie with that draught of hock and soda-water.   1440

181

The coast (I think it was the coast that I
  Was just describing; yes, it *was* the coast)
Lay at this period quiet as the sky,
  The sands untumbled, the blue waves untossed,
And all was stillness save the sea-bird's cry   1445
  And dolphin's leap, and little billow crossed
By some low rock or shelf, that made it fret
Against the boundary it scarcely wet.

182

And forth they wandered, her sire being gone,
  As I have said, upon an expedition;   1450
And mother, brother, guardian, she had none,
  Save Zoe, who, although with due precision
She waited on her lady with the sun,
  Thought daily service was her only mission,
Bringing warm water, wreathing her long tresses,   1455
And asking now and then for cast-off dresses.

183

It was the cooling hour, just when the rounded
  Red sun sinks down behind the azure hill,
Which then seems as if the whole earth it bounded,
  Circling all nature, hushed, and dim, and still,   1460
With the far mountain-crescent half surrounded
  On one side, and the deep sea calm and chill
Upon the other, and the rosy sky,
With one star sparkling through it like an eye.

184

And thus they wandered forth, and, hand in hand,   1465
  Over the shining pebbles and the shells

Glided along the smooth and hardened sand,
  And in the worn and wild receptacles
Worked by the storms, yet worked as it were planned,
  In hollow halls, with sparry roofs and cells,   1470
They turned to rest; and, each clasped by an arm,
Yielded to the deep twilight's purple charm.

185

They looked up to the sky, whose floating glow
  Spread like a rosy ocean, vast and bright;
They gazed upon the glittering sea below,   1475
  Whence the broad moon rose circling into sight;
They heard the wave's splash, and the wind so low,
  And saw each other's dark eyes darting light
Into each other; and, beholding this,
Their lips drew near, and clung into a kiss –   1480

186

A long, long kiss, a kiss of youth and love
  And beauty, all concentrating like rays
Into one focus, kindled from above;
  Such kisses as belong to early days
Where heart and soul and sense in concert move,   1485
  And the blood's lava, and the pulse ablaze,
Each kiss a heartquake – for a kiss's strength,
I think, it must be reckoned by its length.

187

By length I mean duration; theirs endured
  Heaven knows how long – no doubt they never reckoned,
And if they had, they could not have secured
  The sum of their sensations to a second:
They had not spoken, but they felt allured
  As if their souls and lips each other beckoned,
Which, being joined, like swarming bees they clung,   1495
Their hearts the flowers from whence the honey sprung.

188

They were alone, but not alone as they
  Who shut in chambers think it loneliness;
The silent ocean, and the starlight bay,
  The twilight glow, which momently grew less,   1500
The voiceless sands, and dropping caves that lay
  Around them, made them to each other press,
As if there were no life beneath the sky
Save theirs, and that their life could never die.

189

They feared no eyes nor ears on that lone beach,   1505
   They felt no terrors from the night, they were
All in all to each other; though their speech
   Was broken words, they *thought* a language there,
And all the burning tongues the passions teach
   Found in one sigh the best interpreter   1510
Of nature's oracle – first love, that all
Which Eve has left her daughters since her fall.

190

Haidee spoke not of scruples, asked no vows,
   Nor offered any; she had never heard
Of plight and promises to be a spouse,   1515
   Or perils by a loving maid incurred;
She was all which pure ignorance allows,
   And flew to her young mate like a young bird;
And, never having dreamt of falsehood, she
Had not one word to say of constancy.   1520

191

She loved, and was beloved; she adored,
   And she was worshipped; after nature's fashion,
Their intense souls, into each other poured,
   If souls could die, had perished in that passion;
But by degrees their senses were restored,   1525
   Again to be o'ercome, again to dash on;
And, beating 'gainst *his* bosom, Haidee's heart
Felt as if never more to beat apart.

192

Alas, they were so young, so beautiful,
   So lonely, loving, helpless, and the hour   1530
Was that in which the heart is always full,
   And, having o'er itself no further power,
Prompts deeds eternity cannot annul,
   But pays off moments in an endless shower
Of hellfire – all prepared for people giving   1535
Pleasure or pain to one another living.

193

Alas for Juan and Haidee! They were
   So loving and so lovely – till then never,
Excepting our first parents, such a pair
   Had run the risk of being damned for ever;   1540
And Haidee, being devout as well as fair,
   Had doubtless heard about the Stygian river,

Is in its cause as its effect so sweet,
   That Wisdom, ever on the watch to rob   1620
Joy of its alchemy, and to repeat
   Fine truths, even Conscience, too, has a tough job
To make us understand each good old maxim,
So good – I wonder Castlereagh don't tax 'em.

204

And now 'twas done – on the lone shore were plighted   1625
   Their hearts; the stars, their nuptial torches, shed
Beauty upon the beautiful they lighted;
   Ocean their witness, and the cave their bed,
By their own feelings hallowed and united,
   Their priest was Solitude, and they were wed: 1630
And they were happy, for to their young eyes
Each was an angel, and earth paradise.

205

Oh love, of whom great Caesar was the suitor,
   Titus the master, Antony the slave,
Horace, Catullus scholars, Ovid tutor,   1635
   Sappho the sage bluestocking, in whose grave
All those may leap who rather would be neuter
   (Leucadia's rock still overlooks the wave);
Oh love, thou art the very god of evil –
For, after all, we cannot call thee devil.   1640

206

Thou mak'st the chaste connubial state precarious,
   And jestest with the brows of mightiest men:
Caesar and Pompey, Mahomet, Belisarius,
   Have much employed the muse of history's pen;
Their lives and fortunes were extremely various,   1645
   Such worthies Time will never see again;
Yet to these four in three things the same luck holds
They all were heroes, conquerors, and cuckolds.

207

Thou mak'st philosophers; there's Epicurus
   And Aristippus, a material crew!   1650
Who to immoral courses would allure us
   By theories quite practicable too;
If only from the devil they would insure us,
   How pleasant were the maxim (not quite new),
'Eat, drink, and love, what can the rest avail us?' –   1655
So said the royal sage Sardanapalus.

208

But Juan! Had he quite forgotten Julia?
 And should he have forgotten her so soon?
I can't but say it seems to me most truly a
 Perplexing question; but, no doubt, the moon   1660
Does these things for us, and whenever newly a
 Strong palpitation rises, 'tis her boon;
Else how the devil is it that fresh features
Have such a charm for us poor human creatures?

209

I hate inconstancy – I loathe, detest,   1665
 Abhor, condemn, abjure the mortal made
Of such quicksilver clay that in his breast
 No permanent foundation can be laid;
Love, constant love, has been my constant guest,
 And yet last night, being at a masquerade,   1670
I saw the prettiest creature, fresh from Milan,
Which gave me some sensations like a villain.

210

But soon Philosophy came to my aid
 And whispered, 'Think of every sacred tie!'
'I will, my dear Philosophy!' I said,   1675
 'But then her teeth, and then, oh heaven, her eye!
I'll just enquire if she be wife or maid,
 Or neither, out of curiosity.'
'Stop!' cried Philosophy, with air so Grecian
(Though she was masked then as a fair Venetian). 1680

211

'Stop!' So I stopped. But to return: that which
 Men call inconstancy is nothing more
Than admiration due where nature's rich
 Profusion with young beauty covers o'er
Some favoured object; and as in the niche   1685
 A lovely statue we almost adore,
This sort of adoration of the real
Is but a heightening of the *beau-ideal*.

212

'Tis the perception of the beautiful,
 A fine extension of the faculties,   1690
Platonic, universal, wonderful,
 Drawn from the stars, and filtered through the skies,
Without which life would be extremely dull;
 In short, it is the use of our own eyes,

With one or two small senses added, just   1695
To hint that flesh is formed of fiery dust.

213

Yet 'tis a painful feeling, and unwilling,
   For surely if we always could perceive
In the same object graces quite as killing
   As when she rose upon us like an Eve,   1700
'Twould save us many a heartache, many a shilling
   (For we must get them anyhow, or grieve),
Whereas if one sole lady pleased for ever,
How pleasant for the heart, as well as liver!

214

The heart is like the sky, a part of heaven,   1705
   But changes night and day too, like the sky;
Now o'er it clouds and thunder must be driven,
   And darkness and destruction as on high:
But when it hath been scorched, and pierced, and riven,
   Its storms expire in water-drops; the eye   1710
Pours forth at last the heart's blood turned to tears,
Which make the English climate of our years.

215

The liver is the lazaret of bile,
   But very rarely executes its function,
For the first passion stays there such a while,   1715
   That all the rest creep in and form a junction
Like knots of vipers on a dunghill's soil –
   Rage, fear, hate, jealousy, revenge, compunction –
So that all mischiefs spring up from this entrail
Like earthquakes from the hidden fire called 'central'.   1720

216

In the meantime, without proceeding more
   In this anatomy, I've finished now
Two hundred and odd stanzas as before,
   That being about the number I'll allow
Each canto of the twelve, or twenty four;   1725
   And laying down my pen, I make my bow,
Leaving Don Juan and Haidee to plead
For them and theirs with all who deign to read.

Percy Bysshe Shelley
(1792–1822)

To Wordsworth

Poet of nature, thou hast wept to know
That things depart which never may return;
Childhood and youth, friendship and love's first glow
Have fled like sweet dreams, leaving thee to mourn.
These common woes I feel. One loss is mine   5
Which thou too feel'st, yet I alone deplore.
Thou wert as a lone star, whose light did shine
On some frail bark in winter's midnight roar;
Thou hast like to a rock-built refuge stood
Above the blind and battling multitude;   10
In honoured poverty thy voice did weave
Songs consecrate to truth and liberty –
Deserting these, thou leavest me to grieve,
Thus having been, that thou shouldst cease to be.

Hymn to Intellectual Beauty

1

The awful shadow of some unseen Power
  Floats though unseen amongst us, visiting
  This various world with as inconstant wing
As summer winds that creep from flower to flower;
Like moonbeams that behind some piny mountain shower,   5
    It visits with inconstant glance
    Each human heart and countenance;
Like hues and harmonies of evening,
    Like clouds in starlight widely spread,
    Like memory of music fled,   10
    Like aught that for its grace may be
Dear, and yet dearer for its mystery.

2

Spirit of Beauty, that doth consecrate
  With thine own hues all thou dost shine upon
  Of human thought or form – where art thou gone?   15

Why dost thou pass away and leave our state,
This dim vast vale of tears, vacant and desolate?
    Ask why the sunlight not forever
    Weaves rainbows o'er yon mountain river,
Why aught should fail and fade that once is shown,   20
      Why fear and dream, and death and birth
      Cast on the daylight of this earth
      Such gloom, why man has such a scope
For love and hate, despondency and hope?

3

No voice from some sublimer world hath ever   25
  To sage or poet these responses given;
  Therefore the name of God, and ghosts, and heaven
Remain the records of their vain endeavour,
Frail spells, whose uttered charm might not avail to sever,
    From all we hear and all we see,   30
    Doubt, chance, and mutability.
Thy light alone, like mist o'er mountains driven,
    Or music by the night wind sent
    Through strings of some still instrument,
    Or moonlight on a midnight stream,   35
Gives grace and truth to life's unquiet dream.

4

Love, hope, and self-esteem, like clouds depart
  And come, for some uncertain moments lent.
  Man were immortal and omnipotent,
Didst thou, unknown and awful as thou art,   40
Keep with thy glorious train firm state within his heart.
    Thou messenger of sympathies
    That wax and wane in lovers' eyes,
Thou that to human thought art nourishment,
    Like darkness to a dying flame!   45
    Depart not as thy shadow came,
    Depart not lest the grave should be,
Like life and fear, a dark reality.

5

While yet a boy I sought for ghosts, and sped
  Through many a listening chamber, cave and ruin   50
  And starlight wood, with fearful steps pursuing
Hopes of high talk with the departed dead.
I called on poisonous names with which our youth is fed –
    I was not heard, I saw them not
    When musing deeply on the lot   55
Of life, at that sweet time when winds are wooing
    All vital things that wake to bring

News of buds and blossoming.
    Sudden thy shadow fell on me –
I shrieked, and clasped my hands in ecstasy!   60

6

I vowed that I would dedicate my powers
    To thee and thine; have I not kept the vow?
    With beating heart and streaming eyes, even now
I call the phantoms of a thousand hours
Each from his voiceless grave: they have in visioned bowers   65
    Of studious zeal or love's delight
    Outwatched with me the envious night;
They know that never joy illumed my brow
    Unlinked with hope that thou wouldst free
    This world from its dark slavery,   70
    That thou, oh awful loveliness,
Wouldst give whate'er these words cannot express.

7

The day becomes more solemn and serene
    When noon is past; there is a harmony
    In autumn, and a lustre in its sky,   75
Which through the summer is not heard or seen,
As if it could not be, as if it had not been!
    Thus let thy power, which like the truth
    Of nature on my passive youth
Descended, to my onward life supply   80
    Its calm – to one who worships thee,
    And every form containing thee,
    Whom, spirit fair, thy spells did bind
To fear himself, and love all humankind.

Mont Blanc. Lines written in the Vale of Chamouni

I

The everlasting universe of things
Flows through the mind, and rolls its rapid waves,
Now dark, now glittering, now reflecting gloom,
Now lending splendour, where from secret springs
The source of human thought its tribute brings   5
Of waters, with a sound but half its own,
Such as a feeble brook will oft assume
In the wild woods, among the mountains lone,
Where waterfalls around it leap forever,
Where woods and winds contend, and a vast river   10
    Over its rocks ceaselessly bursts and raves.

II

Thus thou, ravine of Arve – dark, deep ravine –
Thou many-coloured, many-voicéd vale,
Over whose pines, and crags, and caverns sail
Fast cloud-shadows and sunbeams: awful scene,   15
Where Power in likeness of the Arve comes down
From the ice gulfs that gird his secret throne,
Bursting through these dark mountains like the flame
Of lightning through the tempest; thou dost lie,
Thy giant brood of pines around thee clinging,   20
Children of elder time, in whose devotion
The chainless winds still come and ever came
To drink their odours, and their mighty swinging
To hear – an old and solemn harmony;
Thine earthly rainbows stretched across the sweep   25
Of the ethereal waterfall, whose veil
Robes some unsculptured image; the strange sleep
Which, when the voices of the desert fail,
Wraps all in its own deep eternity;
Thy caverns echoing to the Arve's commotion –   30
A loud, lone sound no other sound can tame;
Thou art pervaded with that ceaseless motion,
Thou art the path of that unresting sound,
Dizzy ravine! – and when I gaze on thee
I seem as in a trance sublime and strange   35
To muse on my own separate fantasy,
My own, my human mind, which passively
Now renders and receives fast influencings,
Holding an unremitting interchange
With the clear universe of things around;   40
One legion of wild thoughts, whose wandering wings
Now float above thy darkness, and now rest
Where that or thou art no unbidden guest,
In the still cave of the witch Poesy,
Seeking among the shadows that pass by,   45
Ghosts of all things that are, some shade of thee,
Some phantom, some faint image; till the breast
From which they fled recalls them, thou art there!

III

Some say that gleams of a remoter world
Visit the soul in sleep, that death is slumber,   50
And that its shapes the busy thoughts outnumber
Of those who wake and live. I look on high;
Has some unknown omnipotence unfurled
The veil of life and death? Or do I lie
In dream, and does the mightier world of sleep   55
Spread far around and inaccessibly

Its circles? For the very spirit fails,
Driven like a homeless cloud from steep to steep
That vanishes among the viewless gales!
Far, far above, piercing the infinite sky,   60
Mont Blanc appears, still, snowy, and serene.
Its subject mountains their unearthly forms
Pile around it, ice and rock; broad vales between
Of frozen floods, unfathomable deeps
Blue as the overhanging heaven, that spread   65
And wind among the accumulated steeps;
A desert peopled by the storms alone,
Save when the eagle brings some hunter's bone,
And the wolf tracks her there. How hideously
Its shapes are heaped around! – rude, bare, and high,   70
Ghastly, and scarred, and riven. Is this the scene
Where the old earthquake-demon taught her young
Ruin? Were these their toys? Or did a sea
Of fire envelop once this silent snow?
None can reply – all seems eternal now.   75
The wilderness has a mysterious tongue
Which teaches awful doubt, or faith so mild,
So solemn, so serene, that man may be
But for such faith with nature reconciled.
Thou hast a voice, great mountain, to repeal   80
Large codes of fraud and woe – not understood
By all, but which the wise, and great, and good
Interpret, or make felt, or deeply feel.

IV

The fields, the lakes, the forests, and the streams,
Ocean, and all the living things that dwell   85
Within the daedal earth; lightning, and rain,
Earthquake, and fiery flood, and hurricane,
The torpor of the year when feeble dreams
Visit the hidden buds, or dreamless sleep
Holds every future leaf and flower; the bound   90
With which from that detested trance they leap;
The works and ways of man, their death and birth,
And that of him and all that his may be;
All things that move and breathe with toil and sound
Are born and die; revolve, subside and swell.   95
Power dwells apart in its tranquillity
Remote, serene, and inaccessible:
And *this*, the naked countenance of earth
On which I gaze, even these primeval mountains
Teach the adverting mind. The glaciers creep   100

Like snakes that watch their prey, from their far fountains
Slow rolling on; there, many a precipice,
Frost and the sun in scorn of mortal power
Have piled: dome, pyramid, and pinnacle,
A city of death, distinct with many a tower   105
And wall impregnable of beaming ice.
Yet not a city, but a flood of ruin
Is there, that from the boundaries of the sky
Rolls its perpetual stream; vast pines are strewing
Its destined path, or in the mangled soil   110
Branchless and shattered stand; the rocks, drawn down
From yon remotest waste, have overthrown
The limits of the dead and living world,
Never to be reclaimed. The dwelling-place
Of insects, beasts, and birds, becomes its spoil;   115
Their food and their retreat for ever gone,
So much of life and joy is lost. The race
Of man flies far in dread; his work and dwelling
Vanish like smoke before the tempest's stream,
And their place is not known. Below, vast caves   120
Shine in the rushing torrents' restless gleam,
Which from those secret chasms in tumult welling
Meet in the vale; and one majestic river,
The breath and blood of distant lands, forever
Rolls its loud waters to the ocean waves,   125
Breathes its swift vapours to the circling air.

V

Mont Blanc yet gleams on high: the Power is there,
The still and solemn Power of many sights
And many sounds, and much of life and death.
In the calm darkness of the moonless nights,   130
In the lone glare of day, the snows descend
Upon that mountain; none beholds them there,
Nor when the flakes burn in the sinking sun,
Or the starbeams dart through them; winds contend
Silently there, and heap the snow with breath   135
Rapid and strong, but silently! Its home
The voiceless lightning in these solitudes
Keeps innocently, and like vapour broods
Over the snow. The secret strength of things
Which governs thought, and to the infinite dome   140
Of heaven is as a law, inhabits thee!
And what were thou, and earth, and stars, and sea,
If to the human mind's imaginings
Silence and solitude were vacancy?

Ozymandias

I met a traveller from an antique land
Who said, 'Two vast and trunkless legs of stone
Stand in the desert. Near them, on the sand
Half-sunk, a shattered visage lies, whose frown
And wrinkled lip, and sneer of cold command,   5
Tell that its sculptor well those passions read
Which yet survive, stamped on these lifeless things,
The hand that mocked them, and the heart that fed;
And on the pedestal these words appear:
"My name is Ozymandias, King of Kings,   10
Look on my works, ye mighty, and despair!"
Nothing beside remains. Round the decay
Of that colossal wreck, boundless and bare,
The lone and level sands stretch far away.'

The Mask of Anarchy. Written on the Occasion of the Massacre at Manchester

As I lay asleep in Italy
There came a voice from over the Sea,
And with great power it forth led me
To walk in the visions of Poesy.

I met Murder on the way –   5
He had a mask like Castlereagh –
Very smooth he looked, yet grim;
Seven bloodhounds followed him.

All were fat; and well they might
Be in admirable plight,   10
For one by one, and two by two,
He tossed them human hearts to chew,
Which from his wide cloak he drew.

Next came Fraud, and he had on,
Like Eldon, an ermined gown;   15
His big tears, for he wept well,
Turned to millstones as they fell.

And the little children, who
Round his feet played to and fro,
Thinking every tear a gem,   20
Had their brains knocked out by them.

Clothed with the Bible, as with light,
And the shadows of the night,
Like Sidmouth, next Hypocrisy
On a crocodile rode by.   25

And many more Destructions played
In this ghastly masquerade,
All disguised, even to the eyes,
Like Bishops, lawyers, peers, or spies.

Last came Anarchy: he rode   30
On a white horse, splashed with blood;
He was pale even to the lips,
Like Death in the Apocalypse.

And he wore a kingly crown,
And in his grasp a sceptre shone;   35
On his brow this mark I saw –
'I am God, and King, and Law.'

With a pace stately and fast,
Over English land he passed,
Trampling to a mire of blood   40
The adoring multitude.

And a mighty troop around,
With their trampling shook the ground,
Waving each a bloody sword,
For the service of their Lord.   45

And with glorious triumph, they
Rode through England proud and gay,
Drunk as with intoxication
Of the wine of desolation.

O'er fields and towns, from sea to sea,   50
Passed the Pageant swift and free,
Tearing up, and trampling down,
Till they came to London town.

And each dweller, panic-stricken,
Felt his heart with terror sicken   55
Hearing the tempestuous cry
Of the triumph of Anarchy.

For with pomp to meet him came
Clothed in arms like blood and flame,

The hired murderers, who did sing   60
'Thou art God, and Law, and King.

We have waited, weak and lone,
For thy coming, Mighty One!
Our purses are empty, our swords are cold,
Give us glory, and blood, and gold.'   65

Lawyers and priests, a motley crowd,
To the earth their pale brows bowed;
Like a bad prayer, not overloud,
Whispering, 'Thou art Law and God.'

Then all cried with one accord,   70
'Thou art King, and God, and Lord;
Anarchy, to thee we bow,
By thy name made holy now!'

And Anarchy, the Skeleton,
Bowed and grinned to everyone,   75
As well as if his education
Had cost ten millions to the nation.

For he knew the Palaces
Of our Kings were rightly his;
His the sceptre, crown, and globe,   80
And the gold-inwoven robe.

So he sent his slaves before
To seize upon the Bank and Tower,
And was proceeding with intent
To meet his pensioned Parliament;   85

When one fled past, a maniac maid,
And her name was Hope, she said;
But she looked more like Despair,
And she cried out in the air:

'My father Time is weak and grey   90
With waiting for a better day;
She how idiot-like he stands,
Fumbling with his palsied hands!

He has had child after child
And the dust of death is piled   95
Over everyone but me –
Misery, oh, misery!'

Then she lay down in the street,
Right before the horses' feet,
Expecting, with a patient eye,   100
Murder, Fraud and Anarchy.

When between her and her foes
A mist, a light, an image rose,
Small at first, and weak, and frail,
Like the vapour of a vale;   105

Till as clouds grow on the blast,
Like tower-crowned giants striding fast,
And glare with lightnings as they fly,
And speak in thunder to the sky,

It grew – a Shape arrayed in mail   110
Brighter than the viper's scale,
And upborne on wings whose grain
Was as the light of sunny rain.

On its helm, seen far away,
A planet, like the morning's, lay,   115
And those plumes its light rained through
Like a shower of crimson dew.

With step as soft as wind it passed
O'er the heads of men – so fast
That they knew the presence there,   120
And looked – and all was empty air.

As flowers beneath May's footstep waken,
As stars from night's loose hair are shaken,
As waves arise when loud winds call,
Thoughts sprung where'er that step did fall.   125

And the prostrate multitude
Looked – and ankle-deep in blood,
Hope, that maiden most serene,
Was walking with a quiet mien.

And Anarchy, the ghastly birth,   130
Lay dead earth upon the earth;
The Horse of Death, tameless as wind,
Fled, and with his hoofs did grind
To dust the murderers thronged behind.

A rushing light of clouds and splendour,   135
A sense awakening and yet tender,

Was heard and felt – and at its close
These words of joy and fear arose

(As if their own indignant Earth
Which gave the sons of England birth   140
Had felt their blood upon her brow,
And shuddering with a mother's throe

Had turned every drop of blood
By which her face had been bedewed
To an accent unwithstood;   145
As if her heart had cried aloud):

'Men of England, heirs of Glory,
Heroes of unwritten story,
Nurslings of one mighty Mother,
Hopes of her, and one another,   150

Rise like lions after slumber
In unvanquishable number,
Shake your chains to Earth like dew
Which in sleep had fallen on you –
Ye are many; they are few.   155

What is Freedom? Ye can tell
That which slavery is, too well –
For its very name has grown
To an echo of your own.

'Tis to work and have such pay   160
As just keeps life from day to day
In your limbs, as in a cell
For the tyrants' use to dwell.

So that ye for them are made
Loom, and plough, and sword, and spade,   165
With or without your own will bent
To their defence and nourishment.

'Tis to see your children weak
With their mothers pine and peak,
When the winter winds are bleak –   170
They are dying whilst I speak.

'Tis to hunger for such diet
As the rich man in his riot
Casts to the fat dogs that lie
Surfeiting beneath his eye.   175

'Tis to let the Ghost of Gold
Take from toil a thousandfold –
More than ere its substance could
In the tyrannies of old.

Paper coin – that forgery   180
Of the title-deeds, which ye
Hold to something of the worth
Of the inheritance of Earth.

'Tis to be a slave in soul
And to hold no strong control   185
Over your own wills, but be
All that others make of ye.

And at length when ye complain
With a murmur weak and vain,
'Tis to see the Tyrant's crew   190
Ride over your wives and you –
Blood is on the grass like dew.

Then it is to feel revenge
Fiercely thirsting to exchange
Blood for blood and wrong for wrong –   195
Do not thus when ye are strong.

Birds find rest in narrow nest
When weary of their winged quest;
Beasts find fare in woody lair
When storm and snow are in the air.   200

Asses, swine, have litter spread
And with fitting food are fed;
All things have a home but one –
Thou, oh, Englishman, hast none!

This is slavery – savage men   205
Or wild beasts within a den
Would endure not as ye do;
But such ills they never knew.

What art thou Freedom? Oh, could slaves
Answer from their living graves   210
This demand, tyrants would flee
Like a dream's dim imagery.

Thou art not, as impostors say,
A shadow soon to pass away,

A superstition, and a name   215
Echoing from the cave of Fame.

For the labourer thou art bread,
And a comely table spread
From his daily labour come
To a neat and happy home.   220

Thou art clothes, and fire, and food
For the trampled multitude;
No – in countries that are free
Such starvation cannot be
As in England now we see.   225

To the rich thou art a check,
When his foot is on the neck
Of his victim, thou dost make
That he treads upon a snake.

Thou art Justice; ne'er for gold   230
May thy righteous laws be sold
As laws are in England – thou
Shieldst alike the high and low.

Thou art Wisdom – Freemen never
Dream that God will damn for ever   235
All who think those things untrue
Of which Priests make such ado.

Thou art Peace – never by thee
Would blood and treasure wasted be,
As tyrants wasted them, when all   240
Leagued to quench thy flame in Gaul.

What if English toil and blood
Was poured forth, even as a flood?
It availed, oh Liberty!
To dim, but not extinguish thee.   245

Thou art Love – the rich have kissed
Thy feet, and like him following Christ,
Give their substance to the free
And through the rough world follow thee;

Or turn their wealth to arms, and make   250
War for thy beloved sake
On wealth, and war, and fraud – whence they
Drew the power which is their prey.

Science, Poetry, and Thought
Are thy lamps; they make the lot   255
Of the dwellers in a cot
So serene, they curse it not.

Spirit, Patience, Gentleness,
All that can adorn and bless
Art thou – let deeds, not words, express   260
Thine exceeding loveliness.

Let a great Assembly be
Of the fearless and the free
On some spot of English ground
Where the plains stretch wide around.   265

Let the blue sky overhead
The green earth on which ye tread,
All that must eternal be
Witness the solemnity.

From the corners uttermost   270
Of the bounds of English coast;
From every hut, village and town
Where those who live and suffer moan
For others' misery or their own;

From the workhouse and the prison   275
Where pale as corpses newly risen,
Women, children, young and old,
Groan for pain, and weep for cold;

From the haunts of daily life
Where is waged the daily strife   280
With common wants and common cares
Which sows the human heart with tares;

Lastly from the palaces
Where the murmur of distress
Echoes, like the distant sound   285
Of a wind alive around,

Those prison halls of wealth and fashion,
Where some few feel such compassion
For those who groan, and toil, and wail
As must make their brethren pale –   290

Ye who suffer woes untold,
Or to feel, or to behold

Your lost country bought and sold
With a price of blood and gold –

Let a vast Assembly be,   295
And with great solemnity
Declare with measured words that ye
Are, as God has made ye, free.

Be your strong and simple words
Keen to wound as sharpened swords,   300
And wide as targes let them be
With their shade to cover ye.

Let the tyrants pour around
With a quick and startling sound,
Like the loosening of a sea,   305
Troops of armed emblazonry.

Let the charged artillery drive
Till the dead air seems alive
With the clash of clanging wheels,
And the tramp of horses' heels.   310

Let the fixed bayonet
Gleam with sharp desire to wet
Its bright point in English blood,
Looking keen as one for food.

Let the horsemen's scimitars   315
Wheel and flash, like sphereless stars
Thirsting to eclipse their burning
In a sea of death and mourning.

Stand ye calm and resolute,
Like a forest close and mute,   320
With folded arms and looks which are
Weapons of an unvanquished war;

And let Panic, who outspeeds
The career of armed steeds
Pass, a disregarded shade   325
Through your phalanx undismayed.

Let the laws of your own land,
Good or ill, between ye stand
Hand to hand, and foot to foot,
Arbiters of the dispute,   330

The old laws of England – they
Whose reverend heads with age are grey,
Children of a wiser day;
And whose solemn voice must be
Thine own echo – Liberty!   335

On those who first should violate
Such sacred heralds in their state,
Rest the blood that must ensue,
And it will not rest on you.

And if then the tyrants dare,   340
Let them ride among you there,
Slash, and stab, and maim, and hew –
What they like, that let them do.

With folded arms and steady eyes,
And little fear, and less surprise,   345
Look upon them as they slay,
Till their rage has died away.

Then they will return with shame
To the place from which they came,
And the blood thus shed will speak   350
In hot blushes on their cheek.

Every woman in the land
Will point at them as they stand –
They will hardly dare to greet
Their acquaintance in the Street.   355

And the bold, true warriors
Who have hugged Danger in wars
Will turn to those who would be free,
Ashamed of such base company.

And that slaughter to the nation   360
Shall steam up like inspiration,
Eloquent, oracular –
A volcano heard afar.

And these words shall then become
Like oppression's thundered doom   365
Ringing through each heart and brain,
Heard again – again – again.

Rise like lions after slumber
In unvanquishable number;

Shake your chains to earth like dew   370
Which in sleep had fallen on you –
Ye are many, they are few.'

Ode to the West Wind

I

Oh wild west wind, thou breath of autumn's being;
Thou from whose unseen presence the leaves dead
Are driven, like ghosts from an enchanter fleeing,

Yellow, and black, and pale, and hectic red,
Pestilence-stricken multitudes; oh thou   5
Who chariotest to their dark wintry bed

The winged seeds, where they lie cold and low,
Each like a corpse within its grave, until
Thine azure sister of the spring shall blow

Her clarion o'er the dreaming earth, and fill   10
(Driving sweet buds like flocks to feed in air)
With living hues and odours plain and hill –

Wild spirit, which art moving everywhere,
Destroyer and preserver, hear, oh hear!

II

Thou on whose stream, mid the steep sky's commotion,   15
Loose clouds like earth's decaying leaves are shed,
Shook from the tangled boughs of heaven and ocean,

Angels of rain and lightning; there are spread
On the blue surface of thine airy surge,
Like the bright hair uplifted from the head   20

Of some fierce maenad, even from the dim verge
Of the horizon to the zenith's height,
The locks of the approaching storm. Thou dirge

Of the dying year, to which this closing night
Will be the dome of a vast sepulchre,   25
Vaulted with all thy congregated might

Of vapours, from whose solid atmosphere
Black rain, and fire, and hail will burst – oh hear!

III

Thou who didst waken from his summer dreams
The blue Mediterranean, where he lay,   30
Lulled by the coil of his crystalline streams,

Beside a pumice isle in Baiae's bay,
And saw in sleep old palaces and towers
Quivering within the wave's intenser day,

All overgrown with azure moss and flowers   35
So sweet, the sense faints picturing them! Thou
For whose path the Atlantic's level powers

Cleave themselves into chasms, while far below
The sea-blooms and the oozy woods which wear
The sapless foliage of the ocean, know   40

Thy voice, and suddenly grow grey with fear,
And tremble and despoil themselves – oh hear!

IV

If I were a dead leaf thou mightest bear;
If I were a swift cloud to fly with thee;
A wave to pant beneath thy power, and share   45

The impulse of thy strength, only less free
Than thou, oh uncontrollable! If even
I were as in my boyhood, and could be

The comrade of thy wanderings over heaven,
As then, when to outstrip thy skyey speed   50
Scarce seemed a vision; I would ne'er have striven

As thus with thee in prayer in my sore need.
Oh lift me as a wave, a leaf, a cloud!
I fall upon the thorns of life! I bleed!

A heavy weight of hours has chained and bowed   55
One too like thee – tameless, and swift, and proud.

V

Make me thy lyre, even as the forest is:
What if my leaves are falling like its own?
The tumult of thy mighty harmonies

Will take from both a deep autumnal tone,   60
Sweet though in sadness. Be thou, spirit fierce,
My spirit! Be thou me, impetuous one!

Drive my dead thoughts over the universe
Like withered leaves to quicken a new birth!
And, by the incantation of this verse,   65

Scatter, as from an unextinguished hearth
Ashes and sparks, my words among mankind!
Be through my lips to unawakened earth

The trumpet of a prophecy! Oh wind,
If winter comes, can spring be far behind?   70

England in 1819

An old, mad, blind, despised, and dying king;
Princes, the dregs of their dull race, who flow
Through public scorn – mud from a muddy spring;
Rulers who neither see, nor feel, nor know,
But leech-like to their fainting country cling,   5
Till they drop, blind in blood, without a blow.
A people starved and stabbed in th' untilled field;
An army, which liberticide and prey
Makes as a two-edged sword to all who wield;
Golden and sanguine laws which tempt and slay;   10
Religion Christless, Godless – a book sealed;
A senate, time's worst statute, unrepealed –
Are graves from which a glorious phantom may
Burst, to illumine our tempestuous day.

Sonnet

Lift not the painted veil which those who live
Call Life; though unreal shapes be pictured there
And it but mimic all we would believe
With colours idly spread – behind lurk Fear
And Hope, twin destinies, who ever weave   5
Their shadows o'er the chasm, sightless and drear.
I knew one who had lifted it. He sought,
For his lost heart was tender, things to love
But found them not, alas; nor was there aught
The world contains, the which he could approve.   10
Through the unheeding many he did move,
A splendour among shadows, a bright blot
Upon this gloomy scene, a Spirit that strove
For truth, and like the preacher, found it not.

To a Skylark

Hail to thee, blithe spirit!
  Bird thou never wert –
That from heaven, or near it,
  Pourest thy full heart
In profuse strains of unpremeditated art.   5

Higher still and higher
  From the earth thou springest
Like a cloud of fire;
  The blue deep thou wingest,
And singing still dost soar, and soaring ever singest.   10

In the golden lightning
  Of the sunken sun
O'er which clouds are brightning,
  Thou dost float and run
Like an unbodied joy whose race is just begun.   15

The pale purple even
  Melts around thy flight;
Like a star of heaven
  In the broad daylight
Thou art unseen – but yet I hear thy shrill delight,   20

Keen as are the arrows
  Of that silver sphere,
Whose intense lamp narrows
  In the white dawn clear,
Until we hardly see – we feel that it is there.   25

All the earth and air
  With thy voice is loud,
As when night is bare
  From one lonely cloud
The moon rains out her beams – and heaven is overflowed.

What thou art we know not;
  What is most like thee?
From rainbow clouds there flow not
  Drops so bright to see
As from thy presence showers a rain of melody.   35

Like a poet hidden
   In the light of thought,
Singing hymns unbidden,
   Till the world is wrought
To sympathy with hopes and fears it heeded not;   40

Like a high-born maiden
   In a palace-tower,
Soothing her love-laden
   Soul in secret hour,
With music sweet as love, which overflows her bower;   45

Like a glow-worm golden
   In a dell of dew,
Scattering unbeholden
   Its aerial hue
Among the flowers and grass which screen it from the view;   50

Like a rose embowered
   In its own green leaves,
By warm winds deflowered
   Till the scent it gives
Makes faint with too much sweet these heavy-winged thieves; 55

Sound of vernal showers
   On the twinkling grass,
Rain-awakened flowers,
   All that ever was
Joyous and clear and fresh, thy music doth surpass.   60

Teach us, sprite or bird,
   What sweet thoughts are thine;
I have never heard
   Praise of love or wine
That panted forth a flood of rapture so divine: 65

Chorus Hymeneal
   Or triumphal chaunt
Matched with thine would be all
   But an empty vaunt,
A thing wherein we feel there is some hidden want.   70

What objects are the fountains
   Of thy happy strain?
What fields or waves or mountains?
   What shapes of sky or plain?
What love of thine own kind? What ignorance of pain?   75

With thy clear keen joyance
   Languor cannot be –
Shadow of annoyance
   Never came near thee;
Thou lovest, but ne'er knew love's sad satiety.   80

Waking or asleep,
   Thou of death must deem
Things more true and deep
   Than we mortals dream,
Or how could thy notes flow in such a crystal stream?   85

We look before and after,
   And pine for what is not;
Our sincerest laughter
   With some pain is fraught –
Our sweetest songs are those that tell of saddest thought.   90

Yet if we could scorn
   Hate and pride and fear;
If we were things born
   Not to shed a tear,
I know not how thy joy we ever should come near.   95

Better than all measures
   Of delightful sound;
Better than all treasures
   That in books are found –
Thy skill to poet were, thou scorner of the ground!   100

Teach me half the gladness
   That thy brain must know,
Such harmonious madness
   From my lips would flow
The world should listen then, as I am listening now.   105

John Keats (1795–1821)

On First Looking into Chapman's Homer

Much have I travelled in the realms of gold,
  And many goodly states and kingdoms seen;
  Round many western islands have I been
Which bards in fealty to Apollo hold.
Oft of one wide expanse had I been told   5
  That deep-browed Homer ruled as his demesne,
  Yet did I never breathe its pure serene
Till I heard Chapman speak out loud and bold:
Then felt I like some watcher of the skies
  When a new planet swims into his ken;   10
Or like stout Cortez when with eagle eyes
  He stared at the Pacific, and all his men
Looked at each other with a wild surmise –
  Silent, upon a peak in Darien.

Addressed to Haydon

Great spirits now on earth are sojourning:
  He of the cloud, the cataract, the lake,
  Who on Helvellyn's summit, wide awake,
Catches his freshness from archangel's wing;
He of the rose, the violet, the spring,   5
  The social smile, the chain for freedom's sake;
  And lo! whose steadfastness would never take
A meaner sound than Raphael's whispering.
And other spirits there are standing apart
  Upon the forehead of the age to come;   10
These, these will give the world another heart
  And other pulses: hear ye not the hum
Of mighty workings?——
  Listen awhile ye nations, and be dumb.

On Sitting Down to Read King Lear Once Again

Oh golden-tongued Romance, with serene lute!
   Fair plumed siren, queen of far away!
Leave melodizing on this wintry day,
Shut up thine olden pages, and be mute.
Adieu! for, once again, the fierce dispute   5
   Betwixt damnation and impassioned clay
   Must I burn through; once more humbly assay
The bitter-sweet of this Shakespearian fruit.
Chief poet, and ye clouds of Albion,
   Begetters of our deep eternal theme!   10
When through the old oak forest I am gone,
   Let me not wander in a barren dream;
But when I am consumed in the fire,
Give me new phoenix wings to fly at my desire.

Sonnet

When I have fears that I may cease to be
Before my pen has gleaned my teeming brain,
Before high-piled books, in charact'ry,
Hold like rich garners the full-ripened grain;
When I behold, upon the night's starred face,   5
Huge cloudy symbols of a high romance,
And think that I may never live to trace
Their shadows, with the magic hand of chance;
And when I feel, fair creature of an hour,
That I shall never look upon thee more,   10
Never have relish in the fairy power
Of unreflecting love – then on the shore
Of the wide world I stand alone and think,
Till love and fame to nothingness do sink.

The Eve of St Agnes

I

St. Agnes' Eve – ah, bitter chill it was!
The owl, for all his feathers, was a-cold;
The hare limped trembling through the frozen grass,
And silent was the flock in woolly fold.
Numb were the beadsman's fingers, while he told   5

His rosary, and while his frosted breath,
Like pious incense from a censer old,
Seemed taking flight for heaven, without a death,
Past the sweet Virgin's picture, while his prayer he saith.

II

His prayer he saith, this patient, holy man;   10
Then takes his lamp and riseth from his knees,
And back returneth, meagre, barefoot, wan,
Along the chapel aisle by slow degrees.
The sculptured dead on each side seem to freeze,
Imprisoned in black, purgatorial rails;   15
Knights, ladies, praying in dumb orat'ries,
He passeth by; and his weak spirit fails
To think how they may ache in icy hoods and mails.

III

Northward he turneth through a little door,
And scarce three steps ere music's golden tongue   20
Flattered to tears this aged man and poor;
But no – already had his deathbell rung,
The joys of all his life were said and sung –
His was harsh penance on St Agnes' Eve:
Another way he went, and soon among   25
Rough ashes sat he for his soul's reprieve,
And all night kept awake, for sinner's sake to grieve.

IV

That ancient beadsman heard the prelude soft,
And so it chanced, for many a door was wide
From hurry to and fro. Soon, up aloft,   30
The silver, snarling trumpets 'gan to chide;
The level chambers, ready with their pride,
Were glowing to receive a thousand guests;
The carved angels, ever eager-eyed,
Stared, where upon their heads the cornice rests,   35
With hair blown back, and wings put crosswise on their breasts.

V

At length burst in the argent revelry,
With plume, tiara, and all rich array,
Numerous as shadows haunting fairily
The brain, new stuffed in youth, with triumphs gay   40
Of old romance. These let us wish away,
And turn, sole-thoughted, to one lady there,
Whose heart had brooded all that wintry day
On love, and winged St Agnes' saintly care,
As she had heard old dames full many times declare.   45

VI

They told her how, upon St Agnes' Eve,
Young virgins might have visions of delight,
And soft adorings from their loves receive
Upon the honeyed middle of the night,
If ceremonies due they did aright –   50
As, supperless to bed they must retire,
And couch supine their beauties, lily-white;
Nor look behind, nor sideways, but require
Of heaven with upward eyes for all that they desire.

VII

Full of this whim was thoughtful Madeline.   55
The music, yearning like a god in pain,
She scarcely heard; her maiden eyes divine,
Fixed on the floor, saw many a sweeping train
Pass by – she heeded not at all; in vain
Came many a tiptoe, amorous cavalier,   60
And back retired, not cooled by high disdain,
But she saw not; her heart was otherwhere.
She sighed for Agnes' dreams, the sweetest of the year.

VIII

She danced along with vague, regardless eyes;
Anxious her lips, her breathing quick and short.   65
The hallowed hour was near at hand: she sighs
A mid the timbrels and the thronged resort
Of whisperers in anger, or in sport,
Mid looks of love, defiance, hate, and scorn,
Hoodwinked with fairy fancy – all amort,   70
Save to St Agnes and her lambs unshorn,
And all the bliss to be before tomorrow morn.

IX

So, purposing each moment to retire,
She lingered still. Meantime, across the moors
Had come young Porphyro, with heart on fire   75
For Madeline. Beside the portal doors,
Buttressed from moonlight, stands he, and implores
All saints to give him sight of Madeline
But for one moment in the tedious hours,
That he might gaze and worship all unseen,   80
Perchance speak, kneel, touch, kiss – in sooth such things have been.

X

He ventures in – let no buzzed whisper tell;
All eyes be muffled, or a hundred swords
Will storm his heart, love's fev'rous citadel.

For him those chambers held barbarian hordes,   85
Hyena foemen, and hot-blooded lords
Whose very dogs would execrations howl
Against his lineage; not one breast affords
Him any mercy in that mansion foul,
Save one old beldame, weak in body and in soul.   90

XI

Ah, happy chance! The aged creature came,
Shuffling along with ivory-headed wand
To where he stood, hid from the torch's flame
Behind a broad hall-pillar, far beyond
The sound of merriment and chorus bland.   95
He startled her; but soon she knew his face,
And grasped his fingers in her palsied hand,
Saying, 'Mercy, Porphyro! Hie thee from this place;
They are all here tonight, the whole bloodthirsty race!

XII

Get hence! Get hence! There's dwarfish Hildebrand –   100
He had a fever late, and in the fit
He cursed thee and thine, both house and land;
Then there's that old Lord Maurice, not a whit
More tame for his grey hairs. Alas me! Flit,
Flit like a ghost away!' 'Ah, gossip dear,   105
We're safe enough; here in this armchair sit
And tell me how – ' 'Good Saints! Not here, not here;
Follow me, child, or else these stones will be thy bier.'

XIII

He followed through a lowly arched way,
Brushing the cobwebs with his lofty plume,   110
And as she muttered, 'Wel-a – wel-a-day!'
He found him in a little moonlight room,
Pale, latticed, chill, and silent as a tomb.
'Now tell me where is Madeline', said he,
'Oh tell me, Angela, by the holy loom   115
Which none but secret sisterhood may see,
When they St Agnes' wool are weaving piously.'

XIV

'St Agnes! Ah! It is St Agnes' Eve –
Yet men will murder upon holy days!
Thou must hold water in a witch's sieve   120
And be liege-lord of all the elves and fays
To venture so; it fills me with amaze
To see thee, Porphyro! St Agnes' Eve!

God's help! My lady fair the conjuror plays
This very night. Good angels her deceive!   125
But let me laugh awhile, I've mickle time to grieve.'

XV

Feebly she laugheth in the languid moon,
While Porphyro upon her face doth look
Like puzzled urchin on an aged crone
Who keepeth closed a wondrous riddle-book,   130
As spectacled she sits in chimney nook.
But soon his eyes grew brilliant, when she told
His lady's purpose; and he scarce could brook
Tears, at the thought of those enchantments cold,
And Madeline asleep in lap of legends old.   135

XVI

Sudden a thought came like a full blown rose,
Flushing his brow, and in his pained heart
Made purple riot; then doth he propose
A stratagem that makes the beldame start:
'A cruel man and impious thou art –   140
Sweet lady, let her pray, and sleep, and dream
Alone with her good angels, far apart
From wicked men like thee. Go, go! I deem
Thou canst not surely be the same that thou didst seem.'

XVII

'I will not harm her, by all saints I swear',   145
Quoth Porphyro, 'Oh may I ne'er find grace
When my weak voice shall whisper its last prayer,
If one of her soft ringlets I displace,
Or look with ruffian passion in her face;
Good Angela, believe me by these tears,   150
Or I will, even in a moment's space,
Awake, with horrid shout, my foemen's ears,
And beard them, though they be more fanged than wolves and bears.'

XVIII

'Ah, why wilt thou affright a feeble soul?
A poor, weak, palsy-stricken, churchyard thing,   155
Whose passing-bell may ere the midnight toll;
Whose prayers for thee, each morn and evening,
Were never missed!' Thus plaining, doth she bring
A gentler speech from burning Porphyro;
So woeful, and of such deep sorrowing,   160
That Angela gives promise she will do
Whatever he shall wish, betide her weal or woe –

XIX

Which was to lead him, in close secrecy,
Even to Madeline's chamber, and there hide
Him in a closet, of such privacy   165
That he might see her beauty unespied,
And win perhaps that night a peerless bride,
While legioned fairies paced the coverlet
And pale enchantment held her sleepy-eyed.
Never on such a night have lovers met,   170
Since Merlin paid his Demon all the monstrous debt.

XX

'It shall be as thou wishest', said the Dame,
'All cates and dainties shall be stored there
Quickly on this feast-night; by the tambour frame
Her own lute thou wilt see. No time to spare,   175
For I am slow and feeble, and scarce dare
On such a catering trust my dizzy head.
Wait here, my child, with patience; kneel in prayer
The while. Ah! Thou must needs the lady wed,
Or may I never leave my grave among the dead.'   180

XXI

So saying, she hobbled off with busy fear.
The lover's endless minutes slowly passed;
The dame returned, and whispered in his ear
To follow her, with aged eyes aghast
From fright of dim espial. Safe at last,   185
Through many a dusky gallery, they gain
The maiden's chamber, silken, hushed, and chaste,
Where Porphyro took covert, pleased amain.
His poor guide hurried back with agues in her brain.

XXII

Her falt'ring hand upon the balustrade,   190
Old Angela was feeling for the stair,
When Madeline, St Agnes' charmed maid,
Rose, like a missioned spirit, unaware.
With silver taper's light, and pious care,
She turned, and down the aged gossip led   195
To a safe level matting. Now prepare,
Young Porphyro, for gazing on that bed:
She comes, she comes again, like ring-dove frayed and fled.

XXIII

Out went the taper as she hurried in;
Its little smoke, in pallid moonshine, died.   200
She closed the door, she panted, all akin

To spirits of the air, and visions wide –
No uttered syllable, or woe betide!
But to her heart, her heart was voluble,
Paining with eloquence her balmy side,   205
     As though a tongueless nightingale should swell
Her throat in vain, and die, heart-stifled, in her dell.

XXIV

A casement high and triple-arched there was,
All garlanded with carven imag'ries
Of fruits, and flowers, and bunches of knot-grass,   210
And diamonded with panes of quaint device,
Innumerable of stains and splendid dyes,
As are the tiger-moth's deep-damasked wings;
And in the midst, 'mong thousand heraldries,
     And twilight saints, and dim emblazonings,   215
A shielded scutcheon blushed with blood of queens and kings.

XXV

Full on this casement shone the wintry moon,
And threw warm gules on Madeline's fair breast,
As down she knelt for heaven's grace and boon;
Rose-bloom fell on her hands, together pressed,   220
And on her silver cross soft amethyst,
And on her hair a glory, like a saint:
She seemed a splendid angel, newly dressed,
     Save wings, for heaven. Porphyro grew faint;
She knelt, so pure a thing, so free from mortal taint.   225

XXVI

Anon his heart revives; her vespers done,
Of all its wreathed pearls her hair she frees,
Unclasps her warmed jewels one by one,
Loosens her fragrant bodice – by degrees
Her rich attire creeps rustling to her knees.   230
Half-hidden, like a mermaid in seaweed,
Pensive awhile she dreams awake, and sees
     In fancy, fair St Agnes in her bed,
But dares not look behind, or all the charm is fled.

XXVII

Soon, trembling in her soft and chilly nest,   235
In sort of wakeful swoon, perplexed she lay,
Until the poppied warmth of sleep oppressed
Her soothed limbs, and soul fatigued away –
Flown like a thought, until the morrow-day,
     Blissfully havened both from joy and pain,   240
Clasped like a missal where swart paynims pray;

Blinded alike from sunshine and from rain,
As though a rose should shut, and be a bud again.

XXVIII

Stol'n to this paradise, and so entranced,
Porphyro gazed upon her empty dress,   245
And listened to her breathing, if it chanced
To wake into a slumberous tenderness;
Which when he heard, that minute did he bless,
And breathed himself, then from the closet crept,
Noiseless as fear in a wide wilderness –   250
And over the hushed carpet, silent stepped
And 'tween the curtains peeped, where lo! – how fast she slept.

XXIX

Then by the bedside, where the faded moon
Made a dim, silver twilight, soft he set
A table, and, half anguished, threw thereon   255
A cloth of woven crimson, gold, and jet.
Oh for some drowsy Morphean amulet!
The boisterous, midnight, festive clarion,
The kettle-drum, and far-heard clarionet,
Affray his ears, though but in dying tone;   260
The hall door shuts again, and all the noise is gone.

XXX

And still she slept an azure-lidded sleep
In blanched linen, smooth and lavendered,
While he from forth the closet brought a heap
Of candied apple, quince, and plum, and gourd;   265
With jellies soother than the creamy curd,
And lucent syrups tinct with cinnamon;
Manna and dates, in argosy transferred
From Fez; and spiced dainties, every one
From silken Samarkand to cedared Lebanon.   270

XXXI

These delicates he heaped with glowing hand
On golden dishes and in baskets bright
Of wreathed silver; sumptuous they stand
In the retired quiet of the night,
Filling the chilly room with perfume light.   275
'And now, my love, my seraph fair, awake!
Thou art my heaven, and I thine eremite.
Open thine eyes, for meek St Agnes' sake,
Or I shall drowse beside thee, so my soul doth ache.'

XXXII

Thus whispering, his warm, unnerved arm   280
Sank in her pillow. Shaded was her dream
By the dusk curtains; 'twas a midnight charm
Impossible to melt as iced stream.
The lustrous salvers in the moonlight gleam,
Broad golden fringe upon the carpet lies;   285
It seemed he never, never could redeem
From such a steadfast spell his lady's eyes;
So mused awhile, entoiled in woofed fantasies.

XXXIII

Awakening up, he took her hollow lute;
Tumultuous, and, in chords that tenderest be,   290
He played an ancient ditty, long since mute,
In Provence called, 'La belle dame sans mercy',
Close to her ear touching the melody –
Wherewith disturbed, she uttered a soft moan.
He ceased – she panted quick – and suddenly   295
Her blue affrayed eyes wide open shone;
Upon his knees he sank, pale as smooth-sculptured stone.

XXXIV

Her eyes were open, but she still beheld,
Now wide awake, the vision of her sleep –
There was a painful change, that nigh expelled   300
The blisses of her dream so pure and deep.
At which fair Madeline began to weep
And moan forth witless words with many a sigh,
While still her gaze on Porphyro would keep;
Who knelt, with joined hands and piteous eye,   305
Fearing to move or speak, she looked so dreamingly

XXXV

'Ah, Porphyro!' said she, 'but even now
Thy voice was at sweet tremble in mine ear,
Made tuneable with every sweetest vow,
And those sad eyes were spiritual and clear.   310
How changed thou art! How pallid, chill, and drear!
Give me that voice again, my Porphyro,
Those looks immortal, those complainings dear!
Oh leave me not in this eternal woe,
For if thou diest, my love, I know not where to go.'   315

XXXVI

Beyond a mortal man impassioned far
At these voluptuous accents, he arose
Ethereal, flushed, and like a throbbing star
Seen mid the sapphire heaven's deep repose;
Into her dream he melted, as the rose   320
Blendeth its odour with the violet –
Solution sweet. Meantime the frost-wind blows
Like love's alarum pattering the sharp sleet
Against the window-panes; St Agnes' moon hath set.

XXXVII

'Tis dark; quick pattereth the flaw-blown sleet.   325
'This is no dream, my bride, my Madeline!'
'Tis dark; the iced gusts still rave and beat.
'No dream, alas! Alas, and woe is mine!
Porphyro will leave me here to fade and pine.
Cruel! What traitor could thee hither bring?   330
I curse not, for my heart is lost in thine,
Though thou forsakest a deceived thing,
A dove forlorn and lost with sick unpruned wing.'

XXXVIII

'My Madeline! Sweet dreamer! Lovely bride!
Say, may I be for aye thy vassal blessed?   335
Thy beauty's shield, heart-shaped and vermeil dyed?
Ah, silver shrine, here will I take my rest
After so many hours of toil and quest,
A famished pilgrim, saved by miracle.
Though I have found, I will not rob thy nest,   340
Saving of thy sweet self – if thou think'st well
To trust, fair Madeline, to no rude infidel.

XXXIX

Hark! 'Tis an elfin-storm from fairy land,
Of haggard seeming, but a boon indeed.
Arise, arise! The morning is at hand;   345
The bloated wassaillers will never heed.
Let us away, my love, with happy speed;
There are no ears to hear, or eyes to see,
Drowned all in Rhenish and the sleepy mead.
Awake! Arise, my love, and fearless be,   350
For o'er the southern moors I have a home for thee.'

XL

She hurried at his words, beset with fears,
For there were sleeping dragons all around,
At glaring watch, perhaps, with ready spears;

Down the wide stairs a darkling way they found.   355
In all the house was heard no human sound;
A chain-drooped lamp was flickering by each door;
The arras, rich with horseman, hawk, and hound
Fluttered in the besieging wind's uproar,
And the long carpets rose along the gusty floor.   360

XLI
They glide, like phantoms, into the wide hall;
Like phantoms to the iron porch they glide,
Where lay the porter, in uneasy sprawl,
With a huge empty flagon by his side;
The wakeful bloodhound rose and shook his hide,   365
But his sagacious eye an inmate owns.
By one, and one, the bolts full easy slide,
The chains lie silent on the footworn stones –
The key turns, and the door upon its hinges groans.

XLII
And they are gone – aye, ages long ago   370
These lovers fled away into the storm.
That night the Baron dreamt of many a woe,
And all his warrior-guests, with shade and form
Of witch and demon, and large coffin-worm,
Were long be-nightmared. Angela the old   375
Died palsy-twitched, with meagre face deform;
The beadsman, after thousand aves told,
For aye unsought for, slept among his ashes cold.

La Belle Dame Sans Merci: A Ballad

1
Oh what can ail thee, knight-at-arms,
    Alone and palely loitering?
The sedge has withered from the lake,
    And no birds sing.

2
Oh what can ail thee, knight at arms,   5
    So haggard and so woe-begone?
The squirrel's granary is full,
    And the harvest's done.

3
I see a lily on thy brow
    With anguish moist and fever dew,   10
And on thy cheeks a fading rose
    Fast withereth too.

4

I met a lady in the meads,
   Full beautiful – a fairy's child;
Her hair was long, her foot was light,   15
    And her eyes were wild.

5

I made a garland for her head,
   And bracelets too, and fragrant zone;
She looked at me as she did love,
    And made sweet moan.   20

6

I set her on my pacing steed,
   And nothing else saw all day long,
For sidelong would she bend, and sing
    A fairy's song.

7

She found me roots of relish sweet,   25
   And honey wild and manna dew,
And sure in language strange she said,
    'I love thee true'.

8

She took me to her elfin grot
   And there she wept, and sighed full sore,   30
And there I shut her wild wild eyes
    With kisses four.

9

And there she lulled me asleep,
   And there I dreamed – ah, woe betide! –
The latest dream I ever dreamed   35
    On the cold hill's side.

10

I saw pale kings and princes too,
   Pale warriors, death-pale were they all;
They cried, 'La belle dame sans merci
    Hath thee in thrall!'   40

11

I saw their starved lips in the gloam
   With horrid warning gaped wide,
And I awoke and found me here
    On the cold hill's side.

12

And this is why I sojourn here,   45
   Alone and palely loitering,
Though the sedge is withered from the lake,
   And no birds sing.

Ode to Psyche

Oh goddess! Hear these tuneless numbers, wrung
   By sweet enforcement and remembrance dear,
And pardon that thy secrets should be sung
   Even into thine own soft-conched ear.
Surely I dreamt today, or did I see   5
   The winged Psyche with awakened eyes?
I wandered in a forest thoughtlessly,
   And, on the sudden, fainting with surprise,
Saw two fair creatures, couched side by side
   In deepest grass, beneath the whisp'ring roof   10
   Of leaves and trembled blossoms, where there ran
      A brooklet, scarce espied.
Mid hushed, cool-rooted flowers, fragrant-eyed,
   Blue, silver-white, and budded Tyrian,
They lay calm-breathing on the bedded grass;   15
   Their arms embraced, and their pinions too;
   Their lips touched not, but had not bade adieu,
As if disjoined by soft-handed slumber,
And ready still past kisses to outnumber
   At tender eye-dawn of aurorean love.   20
      The winged boy I knew;
   But who wast thou, oh happy, happy dove?
      His Psyche true!

Oh latest born and loveliest vision far
   Of all Olympus' faded hierarchy!   25
Fairer than Phoebe's sapphire-regioned star,
   Or Vesper, amorous glow-worm of the sky;
Fairer than these, though temple thou hast none,
      Nor altar heaped with flowers;
Nor virgin-choir to make delicious moan   30
      Upon the midnight hours;
No voice, no lute, no pipe, no incense sweet
   From chain-swung censer teeming;
No shrine, no grove, no oracle, no heat
   Of pale-mouthed prophet dreaming.   35

Oh brightest! though too late for antique vows,
   Too, too late for the fond believing lyre,

When holy were the haunted forest boughs,
  Holy the air, the water and the fire;
Yet even in these days so far retired   40
  From happy pieties, thy lucent fans,
  Fluttering among the faint Olympians,
I see, and sing, by my own eyes inspired.
So let me be thy choir, and make a moan
         Upon the midnight hours;   45
Thy voice, thy lute, thy pipe, thy incense sweet
  From swinged censer teeming;
Thy shrine, thy grove, thy oracle, thy heat
  Of pale-mouthed prophet dreaming.

Yes, I will be thy priest, and build a fane   50
  In some untrodden region of my mind,
Where branched thoughts, new grown with pleasant pain,
  Instead of pines shall murmur in the wind;
Far, far around shall those dark-clustered trees
  Fledge the wild-ridged mountains steep by steep;   55
And there by zephyrs, streams, and birds, and bees,
  The moss-lain dryads shall be lulled to sleep;
And in the midst of this wide quietness
A rosy sanctuary will I dress
With the wreathed trellis of a working brain,   60
  With buds, and bells, and stars without a name,
With all the gardener Fancy e'er could feign,
  Who, breeding flowers, will never breed the same:
And there shall be for thee all soft delight
  That shadowy thought can win –   65
A bright torch, and a casement ope at night,
  To let the warm love in!

Ode to a Nightingale

1

My heart aches, and a drowsy numbness pains
  My sense, as though of hemlock I had drunk,
Or emptied some dull opiate to the drains
  One minute past, and Lethe-wards had sunk;
'Tis not through envy of thy happy lot,   5
  But being too happy in thine happiness,
    That thou, light-winged dryad of the trees,
      In some melodious plot
Of beechen green, and shadows numberless,
  Singest of summer in full-throated ease.   10

2

Oh for a draught of vintage! that hath been
   Cooled a long age in the deep-delved earth,
Tasting of flora and the country green,
   Dance, and Provençal song, and sunburnt mirth!
Oh for a beaker full of the warm south,   15
   Full of the true, the blushful Hippocrene,
     With beaded bubbles winking at the brim,
       And purple-stained mouth;
   That I might drink, and leave the world unseen,
     And with thee fade away into the forest dim –   20

3

Fade far away, dissolve, and quite forget
   What thou among the leaves hast never known,
The weariness, the fever, and the fret
   Here, where men sit and hear each other groan;
Where palsy shakes a few, sad, last grey hairs,   25
   Where youth grows pale, and spectre-thin, and dies;
     Where but to think is to be full of sorrow
       And leaden-eyed despairs;
   Where Beauty cannot keep her lustrous eyes,
     Or new Love pine at them beyond tomorrow.   30

4

Away! Away! For I will fly to thee,
   Not charioted by Bacchus and his pards,
But on the viewless wings of Poesy,
   Though the dull brain perplexes and retards,
Already with thee! Tender is the night,   35
   And haply the Queen Moon is on her throne,
     Clustered around by all her starry fays;
       But here there is no light
Save what from heaven is with the breezes blown
   Through verdurous glooms and winding mossy ways.   40

5

I cannot see what flowers are at my feet,
   Nor what soft incense hangs upon the boughs,
But, in embalmed darkness, guess each sweet
   Wherewith the seasonable month endows
The grass, the thicket, and the fruit-tree wild,   45
   White hawthorn, and the pastoral eglantine,
     Fast-fading violets covered up in leaves,
       And mid-May's eldest child,
   The coming musk-rose, full of dewy wine,
     The murmurous haunt of flies on summer eves.   50

6

Darkling I listen; and for many a time
    I have been half in love with easeful Death,
Called him soft names in many a mused rhyme,
    To take into the air my quiet breath;
Now more than ever seems it rich to die,   55
    To cease upon the midnight with no pain,
        While thou art pouring forth thy soul abroad
            In such an ecstasy!
        Still wouldst thou sing, and I have ears in vain –
            To thy high requiem become a sod.   60

7

Thou wast not born for death, immortal bird!
    No hungry generations tread thee down;
The voice I hear this passing night was heard
    In ancient days by emperor and clown:
Perhaps the self-same song that found a path   65
    Through the sad heart of Ruth, when, sick for home,
        She stood in tears amid the alien corn;
            The same that oft-times hath
        Charmed magic casements, opening on the foam
            Of perilous seas, in fairy lands forlorn.   70

8

Forlorn! The very word is like a bell
    To toll me back from thee to my sole self!
Adieu! The fancy cannot cheat so well
    As she is famed to do, deceiving elf.
Adieu! Adieu! Thy plaintive anthem fades   75
    Past the near meadows, over the still stream,
        Up the hillside, and now 'tis buried deep
            In the next valley-glades:
        Was it a vision, or a waking dream?
            Fled is that music – do I wake or sleep?   80

Ode on a Grecian Urn

1

Thou still unravished bride of quietness,
    Thou foster-child of silence and slow time,
Sylvan historian, who canst thus express
    A flowery tale more sweetly than our rhyme –
What leaf-fringed legend haunts about thy shape   5
    Of deities or mortals, or of both,
        In Tempe or the dales of Arcady?
        What men or gods are these? What maidens loath?

What mad pursuit? What struggle to escape?
    What pipes and timbrels? What wild ecstasy?   10

2

Heard melodies are sweet, but those unheard
    Are sweeter; therefore, ye soft pipes, play on –
Not to the sensual ear, but, more endeared,
    Pipe to the spirit ditties of no tone:
Fair youth, beneath the trees, thou canst not leave   15
    Thy song, nor ever can those trees be bare;
        Bold lover, never, never canst thou kiss,
Though winning near the goal – yet do not grieve;
    She cannot fade, though thou hast not thy bliss,
        For ever wilt thou love, and she be fair!   20

3

Ah, happy, happy boughs! that cannot shed
    Your leaves, nor ever bid the spring adieu;
And, happy melodist, unwearied,
    For ever piping songs for ever new;
More happy love, more happy, happy love!   25
    For ever warm and still to be enjoyed,
        For ever panting and for ever young;
All breathing human passion far above,
    That leaves a heart high-sorrowful and cloyed,
        A burning forehead, and a parching tongue.   30

4

Who are these coming to the sacrifice?
    To what green altar, oh mysterious priest,
Lead'st thou that heifer lowing at the skies,
    And all her silken flanks with garlands dressed?
What little town by river or seashore,   35
    Or mountain-built with peaceful citadel,
        Is emptied of this folk, this pious morn?
And, little town, thy streets for evermore
    Will silent be, and not a soul to tell
        Why thou art desolate, can e'er return.   40

5

Oh Attic shape! Fair attitude! With brede
    Of marble men and maidens overwrought,
With forest branches and the trodden weed;
    Thou, silent form, dost tease us out of thought
As doth eternity. Cold Pastoral!   45
    When old age shall this generation waste,
        Thou shalt remain, in midst of other woe
Than ours, a friend to man, to whom thou say'st,

'Beauty is truth, truth beauty'; that is all
  Ye know on earth, and all ye need to know.   50

Ode on Melancholy

1

No, no, go not to Lethe, neither twist
  Wolfsbane, tight-rooted, for its poisonous wine;
Nor suffer thy pale forehead to be kissed
  By nightshade, ruby grape of Proserpine;
Make not your rosary of yew-berries,   5
  Nor let the beetle, nor the death-moth be
    Your mournful Psyche, nor the downy owl
A partner in your sorrow's mysteries;
  For shade to shade will come too drowsily,
    And drown the wakeful anguish of the soul.   10

2

But when the melancholy fit shall fall
  Sudden from heaven like a weeping cloud,
That fosters the droop-headed flowers all,
  And hides the green hill in an April shroud;
Then glut thy sorrow on a morning rose,   15
  Or on the rainbow of the salt sand-wave,
    Or on the wealth of globed peonies;
Or if thy mistress some rich anger shows,
  Imprison her soft hand, and let her rave,
    And feed deep, deep upon her peerless eyes.   20

3

She dwells with Beauty – Beauty that must die;
  And Joy, whose hand is ever at his lips
Bidding adieu; and aching Pleasure nigh,
  Turning to poison while the bee-mouth sips.
Aye, in the very temple of Delight   25
  Veiled Melancholy has her sovran shrine,
    Though seen of none save him whose strenuous tongue
Can burst Joy's grape against his palate fine;
  His soul shall taste the sadness of her might,
    And be among her cloudy trophies hung.   30

Ode on Indolence

They toil not, neither do they spin.

1

One morn before me were three figures seen,
  With bowed necks and joined hands, side-faced;
And one behind the other stepped serene,
  In placid sandals and in white robes graced;
They passed, like figures on a marble urn,   5
  When shifted round to see the other side;
    They came again, as when the urn once more
Is shifted round, the first-seen shades return –
  And they were strange to me, as may betide
    With vases, to one deep in Phidian lore.   10

2

How is it, shadows, that I knew ye not?
  How came ye muffled in so hush a masque?
Was it a silent deep-disguised plot
  To steal away, and leave without a task
My idle days? Ripe was the drowsy hour,   15
  The blissful cloud of summer indolence
    Benumbed my eyes; my pulse grew less and less;
Pain had no sting, and pleasure's wreath no flower –
  Oh why did ye not melt, and leave my sense
    Unhaunted quite of all but – nothingness?   20

3

A third time passed they by, and, passing, turned
  Each one the face a moment whiles to me;
Then faded, and to follow them I burned
  And ached for wings, because I knew the three;
The first was a fair maid, and Love her name;   25
  The second was Ambition, pale of cheek
    And ever watchful with fatigued eye;
The last, whom I love more, the more of blame
  Is heaped upon her, maiden most unmeek,
    I knew to be my demon Poesy.   30

4

They faded, and, forsooth, I wanted wings!
  Oh folly! What is love? And where is it?
And, for that poor ambition – it springs
  From a man's little heart's short fever-fit;
For Poesy! No, she has not a joy –   35
  At least for me – so sweet as drowsy noons,
    And evenings steeped in honeyed indolence.
Oh for an age so sheltered from annoy,
  That I may never know how change the moons,
    Or hear the voice of busy common sense!   40

5

A third time came they by – alas, wherefore?
  My sleep had been embroidered with dim dreams;
My soul had been a lawn besprinkled o'er
  With flowers, and stirring shades, and baffled beams;
The morn was clouded, but no shower fell,   45
  Though in her lids hung the sweet tears of May;
    The open casement pressed a new-leaved vine,
Let in the budding warmth and throstle's lay –
  Oh shadows, 'twas a time to bid farewell!
    Upon your skirts had fallen no tears of mine.   50

6

So ye three ghosts, adieu! Ye cannot raise
  My head cool-bedded in the flowery grass,
For I would not be dieted with praise –
  A pet-lamb in a sentimental farce!
Fade softly from my eyes, and be once more   55
  In masque-like figures on the dreamy urn;
    Farewell! I yet have visions for the night,
And for the day faint visions there is store.
  Vanish, ye phantoms, from my idle sprite,
    Into the clouds, and never more return!   60

To Autumn

1

Season of mists and mellow fruitfulness,
  Close bosom-friend of the maturing sun,
Conspiring with him how to load and bless
  With fruit the vines that round the thatch-eaves run;
To bend with apples the mossed cottage-trees,   5
  And fill all fruit with ripeness to the core;
    To swell the gourd, and plump the hazel shells
With a sweet kernel; to set budding more,

And still more, later flowers for the bees,
Until they think warm days will never cease,   10
For summer has o'er-brimmed their clammy cells.

2

Who hath not seen thee oft amid thy store?
Sometimes whoever seeks abroad may find
Thee sitting careless on a granary floor,
Thy hair soft-lifted by the winnowing wind;   15
Or on a half-reaped furrow sound asleep,
Drowsed with the fume of poppies, while thy hook
Spares the next swath and all its twined flowers;
And sometimes like a gleaner thou dost keep
Steady thy laden head across a brook;   20
Or by a cider-press, with patient look,
Thou watchest the last oozings hours by hours.

3

Where are the songs of spring? Aye, where are they?
Think not of them, thou hast thy music too –
While barred clouds bloom the soft-dying day,   25
And touch the stubble-plains with rosy hue;
Then in a wailful choir the small gnats mourn
Among the river sallows, borne aloft
Or sinking as the light wind lives or dies;
And full-grown lambs loud bleat from hilly bourn,   30
Hedge-crickets sing, and now with treble soft
The redbreast whistles from a garden-croft,
And gathering swallows twitter in the skies.

Bright star, would I were steadfast as thou art

Bright star, would I were steadfast as thou art –
Not in lone splendour hung aloft the night
And watching, with eternal lids apart,
Like nature's patient, sleepless eremite,
The moving waters at their priestlike task   5
Of pure ablution round earth's human shores,
Or gazing on the new soft-fallen mask
Of snow upon the mountains and the moors;
No – yet still steadfast, still unchangeable,
Pillowed upon my fair love's ripening breast,   10
To feel for ever its soft swell and fall,
Awake for ever in a sweet unrest,
Still, still to hear her tender-taken breath,
And so live ever – or else swoon to death.

Index of Titles and First Lines